Copyright 2014 @ Roho Publishing. All rights reserved. Printed in the United States.

ISBN:978-0-9894338-5-3
Cover Design Jenna Stanbrough
Cover Photo: Mark Stanbrough

Roho Publishing
4040 Graphic Arts Road
Emporia, KS 66801

www.rohopublishing.com

About Roho Publishing

When Kip Keino defeated Jim Ryun in the 1968 Olympic Games at 1500 meters he credited the win to "Roho." Roho is the Swahili word for spirit demonstrated through extraordinary strength and courage. The type of courage and strength that can be summoned up from deep within that will allow you to meet your goals and overcome the challenges in life. Roho Publishing focuses on the spirit of sport and is designed to inspire, encourage, motivate, and teach valuable life lessons.

Dedication

To the ordinary person who works hard every day. Your efforts and extraordinary desire makes you a hero.

Acknowledgements

To my daughter Jenna who designed the cover, and did the page layouts and editing. My right hand person, whose great effort gets the job done.

To my daughters, Bethany and Leslie for their reviews of the manuscript.

To my wife, Wendy, my life-time motivation.

To my parents, my heroes.

Title	Hero	Page
Introduction		6
Across The Channel	Gertrude Ederle	8
Bad Luck Can Kick You Forward	Ernest Hemmingway	9
Believe and Lead	Winston Churchill	10
Believe, Believe, Believe	Billy Mills	11
Best Effort	John Wooden	12
Blind and In Prison	John Milton	13
Bouncing Back	Charles Goodyear	14
Breaking Through Barriers	Roger Bannister	15
Bulb Burns Bright	Thomas Edison	16
Composing a Masterpiece	Beethoven	17
Crazy Horse	Korczak Ziolkowski	18
Desire to Serve	Golda Meir	19
Determination	John Roebling	20
Dream for a World of Hope	Terry Fox	21
Father's Love	Team Hoyt	22
Find A Way	Diana Nyad	23
Gazelle	Wilma Rudolph	24
Golden Arches	Ray Kroc	25
Hard Work Reaps Rewards	Ewing Kauffman	26
Helping Through Medical Discoveries	Louis Pasteur	27
I Am an Alcoholic	Bill Wilson	28
I Can Do Something	Helen Keller	29
I Have a Dream	Martin Luther King Jr.	30
Imagination Runs Wild	Theodore Geisel	31
Iron Man	Glenn Cunningham	32
I Will Do My Best	James West	33
Keeping the Faith	J.K. Rowling	34
Keep on Knocking	Harlan Sanders	35

Title	Hero	Page
Kiss of Kindness	Milton Hershey	36
Laughed at His Paper	Allen Neuharth	37
Leading Through Challenges	Franklin Roosevelt	38
Learning is Relative	Albert Einstein	39
Life Tastes Good	John Pemberton	40
Long Walk to Freedom	Nelson Mandela	41
Making a Difference	Albert Nobel	42
Mistakes May Turn Out Well	George Crum	43
Mount Everest - I'm Still Growing	Edmund Hillary	44
Musical Genius	Ray Charles	45
Never Too Late	Grandma Moses	46
No Limits	George Dantzig	47
Overcoming Dyslexia	Tom Cruise	48
Persistence of Lincoln	Abraham Lincoln	49
Playing With One Hand	Jim Abbott	50
Real Horror Story	Stephen King	51
Revolutionary Vision	Henry Ford	52
Rough Rider	Theodore Roosevelt	53
Rough Road to Success	Oprah Winfrey	54
Soul Surfer	Bethany Hamilton	55
Starry Starry Night	Vincent van Gogh	56
Successful Act	Sydney Poitier	57
Trailblazing	Sam Walton	58
Triumph of an American Dreamer	Walt Disney	59
This Seat Is Mine	Rosa Parks	60
Turning Bad Luck into Good Luck	Charles Walgreen	61
Unlock Your Mind	Harry Houdini	62
Wear the Red	Lakota Indians	63
Wonder of It All	Stevie Wonder	64
World's Toughest Race	Cliff Young	65

Title	Hero	Page
While I Pondered Weak and Weary	Edgar Allan Poe	66
Resources		67
About the Author		74

Introduction

People are in need of heroes today more than at any other time in our history. We are often bombarded with everyday media focusing on the negative messages of violence, drugs, terrorism; and the list goes on with anything that is an attention grabber and will sell. The heroes profiled in the following stories display the drive, motivation, and dedication to overcome adversity and numerous challenges to reach their goals. Their stories teach the values of self-discipline, responsibility, accountability, and loyalty. They demonstrate the qualities necessary to be successful in life—good character, integrity, a strong work ethic, dedication, and perseverance.

In developing character it is important that we use positive thoughts. These positive thoughts can be fueled by positive stories. The stories of heroes who have overcome adversity and the challenges of life can have a very powerful influence in making a life-changing impact. An ancient philosophy handed down through the ages is that a person becomes what they think. It is a philosophy characterized by the idea that a person's character is the outward expression of their inner thoughts. James Allen in his book, *As a Man Thinketh,* states, "All that a man achieves or fails to achieve is the direct results of his own thoughts."

Stories are memorable; they lodge in the long-term memory. American psychologist Jerome Bruner (1990) investigated different modes of thinking and found that people are 20 times more likely to remember information in the form of a story than as a set of disconnected facts. As Rudyard Kipling stated, "If history were taught in the form of stories, it would never be forgotten."

Reading and listening to stories require a complex human activity that uses the whole-brain function. The left brain is the pattern seeker, the side of the brain that processes the language sequentially and analyzes the character and plot. It focuses on the content or "what" of the story. The right brain focuses on the "why" and puts the information into context. It sees the big picture and visualizes. The right brain takes us out of our normal thinking mode and tells us how the story relates to us.

When we listen and relate to information in the shape of a story, our imagination starts telling us a secondary, almost parallel story that has unique relevance to us. It connects with our emotions and mobilizes us into action. Most of this happens in our subconscious mind and we don't even realize that we have been influenced.

During difficult times it becomes easy to get stuck in the same negative thinking pattern. Stories can lift individuals or groups out of the negative mindset, and allow them to step back and see things in a different, more positive way, maybe in a way they have never imagined.

You're bound to find motivation and encouragement from the stories, affirmation, quotes, and questions in *Developing Character Though Motivational Heroes*, no matter your walk of life. Hopefully, you receive pleasure and inspiration from these pages and develop the strong, positive character that will lead to a long, happy, highly productive, and positive life.

There are many ways the stories and questions can be used. Here are 10 suggestions:

1. Post on bulletin board for all to read.

2. Distribute event specific stories.

3. The leader reads the story and then a group discussion takes place.

4. Individuals are assigned to read stories to a group. Group discussion takes place after the story is read.

5. An individual reads the story within a small group. Small group discussion takes place after the story is read.

6. A group discusses questions during an activity.

7. Stories can be read during a break in activity.

8. Questions can be discussed during a break in activity.

9. Reading of the story and discussion on stories can take place at the end of an activity.

10. Individuals can be given a story to help motivate them under specific situations such as when injured, performance is sub-par, or a person is depressed.

Across the Channel

In the 1924 Olympics, Gertrude (Gertie) Ederle won a gold medal in the 4x100-meter relay and bronze medals in the 100 and 400-meter freestyle races. At the time, the longest swimming event for women in the Olympics was just 400 meters. The idea of women swimming long distance was unheard of and deemed impossible. In fact, it was an era where many found it difficult to take female athletes seriously. But Gertrude Ederle had a dream and was serious about swimming across the English Channel, a distance of 21 miles.

Five men had swum across the English Channel previously but they had all used the breast stroke. Gertrude planned to use the front crawl, a stroke considered too strenuous for a distance swim. Her critics laughed at her goals. She first tried crossing the English Channel in 1925, but after nine hours she was forced to quit.

Nineteen-year-old Gertrude, smeared with sheep grease to protect her from the frigid water, slipped into the English Channel at Cap Grix-Ne, France, on the morning of August 6, 1926. Twice during the swim, her trainer, aboard the boat that accompanied her, suggested that she give up her quest. During the last few hours, she had to swim in a rough sea, the tide pushing strongly against her and the ocean spray stinging her face. The rough seas took her off course and she actually swam 35 miles instead of the intended 21.

With a never give-up attitude, her determination to succeed took her across the English Channel. The swim took 14 hours and 31 minutes; one hour and 21 minutes faster than any man had ever swum it.

Gertrude Ederle's determined effort and extraordinary desire had a profound effect on women's sports. She was one of the first women that helped disprove the belief that women were physically inferior to men. Her crossing of the English Channel challenged perceptions of female athletes, inspiring countless women to take up various sports with a confidence to step up to meet the challenge.

Affirmation: I believe I will achieve.

To think about:

1. Gertrude Ederle helped prove women could accomplish what was once considered "men only" goals. How does a positive mindset affect performance?

2. Gertie failed on her first attempt. How do you take failure and turn it into success?

3. Gertie was blown off her original path and had to swim an additional 14 miles. How do you adjust when you appear to be getting off track?

When somebody tells me I cannot do something, that's when I do it. -Gertrude Ederle

Bad Luck Can Kick You Forward

Ernest Hemmingway won the Nobel Prize for Literature in 1954. His personality and constant pursuit of adventure—bullfighting in Spain, African safaris, deep-sea diving in Florida, and surviving multiple plane crashes—became legendary. His iconic style still influences writers today. However, if not for bad luck, the world may never have known Ernest Hemmingway.

Ernest Hemingway was in Switzerland, on assignment, when he met an editor who asked to see some of his work. At that point, none of his fiction had been published. His wife, Hadley, was in Paris, where they were living at the time. She packed up all of Ernest's manuscripts in a suitcase and planned to take them to him in Switzerland. The suitcase contained many stories Ernest had polished to perfection, which he'd been planning to publish in a book. While at the train station, she went to get a drink of water, leaving the suitcase unattended on the train. When she came back, the suitcase was gone.

Thinking she was being thorough, Hadley had packed both the originals and their carbons in the suitcase. Ernest was devastated and couldn't conceive of redoing his work. All those months of arduous writing were simply wasted.

When he told his friend and poet Ezra Pound about the bad luck, Pound called it a stroke of good fortune! Pound assured Ernest that when he rewrote the stories, he would forget the weak parts; only the best material would reappear. He encouraged the aspiring author to start over with a sense of optimism and confidence.

With time pressing to replace those vanished words in his bid to become a respected writer, Ernest adopted and adapted the lean prose style for which he became famous. Using that style he would go on to publish numerous novels and become a major figure in American literature.

Affirmation: I "bring it" when there is a challenge.

To think about:

1. Ernest had to take steps backwards to go forward. Have you ever had to redo work? Did the do-over turn out better than the original?

2. Ernest almost gave up at one point after losing his manuscripts, but changed his style of writing. How does having a goal help you to be kicked forward?

3. How can you view bad luck as being kicked forward?

Don't pray for fewer problems, pray for more skills. Don't ask for smaller challenges, ask for greater wisdom. Don't look for an easy way out, look for the best possible outcome. When life gives you a kick, let it kick you forward. -Steve Goodier

Believe and Lead

Winston Churchill performed poorly at the first two schools he attended because of his stuttering problem. He was sent to a boarding school near London and eventually joined the Harrow Rifle Corps, which put him on a path to a military career.

Initially, it appeared that the military was not a good move for Churchill. It took him three tries to pass the exam for military college. After a brief military career, he left the army and worked as a war correspondent. While reporting on the Boer War in South Africa, he was taken prisoner, but escaped, traveling almost 300 miles to Portuguese territory in Mozambique.

In 1900, he became a member of Parliament and when World War II broke out he became the Prime Minister of England. For much of 1940, London was under constant German air attack. Churchill, nevertheless, refused Hitler's offers of peace, believing what very few believed, democracy would win. His hope that the United States would come to the aid of Great Britain came true when Japan attacked Pearl Harbor and the United States joined World War II as a British ally.

Winston Churchill did not merely hate tyranny, he despised it. Known for his powerful and rousing speeches, he became one of the most influential political leaders in history. The greatest of all Britain's war leaders not only led his country, but strengthened the world's faith in the moral superiority of democracy and the inevitability of its triumph.

Affirmation: I will lead based upon what I believe.

To think about:

1. Winston stayed true to his beliefs and values when many doubted him. What are the major things that you value?

2. Because of his solid belief in democracy, Winston was a great leader. What are the qualities that make you a leader?

3. On a scale of 1-10 (1 low and 10 high), what kind of role model are you?

A pessimist sees the difficulty in every opportunity; an optimist sees the opportunity in every difficulty. -Winston Churchill

Believe-Believe-Believe

Billy Mills, a Native American (Oglala Lakota), was raised on the Pine Ridge Indian Reservation in South Dakota. He was orphaned at the age of 12. Billy took up running while attending the Haskell Institute in Lawrence, Kansas. He attended the University of Kansas and earned All-America cross country honors three times, and in 1960, he won the individual title in the Big Eight Cross Country Championships. Billy helped lead the University of Kansas track team to the 1959 and 1960 Outdoor National Championships.

Photo Courtesy of Kansas Athletics

Billy went on to become a lieutenant in the United States Marine Corps. After giving up running for a while, he returned to the sport to qualify for the 1964 Summer Olympics in Tokyo in the 10,000-meter run and the marathon. On October 14, 1964, 38 runners competed in the 10,000-meter final at the Tokyo Olympics. Billy had a 10,000-meter best of 29:10.4, and was virtually unknown and not expected to be a medal contender. However, Billy, who had faced discrimination and difficult times his entire life, believed in himself. As he trained for the Olympic Games he visualized himself running the race over and over. In his mind, he saw himself running with the leaders and winning. He repeated over and over to himself the affirmation, "believe-believe-believe."

The race favorite, world-record holder Ron Clarke of Australia, led most of the race with a quick pace. With one lap remaining, Clarke had dropped all his main rivals, but he still had two athletes with him. Billy Mills and Mohamed Gammoudi of Tunisia were both relatively unknown and both running much faster than they ever had before. The three were hindered by lapped runners on the last lap who made no effort to let them through on the inside. In the back straight, Clarke bumped Billy, pushing him to the outside lanes and causing him to drop back about four meters. At this point, Billy focused on his affirmations, "believe-believe-believe," as Gammoudi and Clarke sprinted for the finish. Gammoudi had shaken off Clarke and seemed to have the race won with 50 meters to go before Billy came storming past both of them to win the gold medal. Billy's winning time of 28:24.4 was a personal record by 50 seconds and a new Olympic record. The race has been called the greatest upset in Olympic history and his victory remains the only Olympic 10,000-meter win in U.S. Olympic history.

Affirmation: I believe in myself.

To think about:

1. Why was Billy Mills' race so surprising?

2. How did Billy prepare himself mentally to run in the Olympic Games?

3. How can you apply the story of Billy Mills to help you as a person?

Every passion has its destiny. -Billy Mills

Best Effort

John Wooden grew up on a farm in Ohio with his three brothers using a tomato basket and a makeshift ball consisting of old rags. As a high school junior, John led his team to a state title. He went to Purdue, where he captained the basketball team and led the Boilermakers to two Big Ten titles. In 1932, he was named college basketball's Player of the Year and Purdue was voted the national champion (before the national tournament was started).

John was offered money to play pro basketball but decided to put his education to use. He became a high school teacher and coach, coaching several sports. John's teaching and coaching career was interrupted by World War II, where he served in the Navy. After the war, he became the athletic director, basketball, and baseball coach at Indiana State. After two seasons, John was hired by UCLA. At the time, UCLA had no on-campus arena and for his first 17 years, they played their home games in their tiny practice facility or off-campus.

With an emphasis on attention to details and discipline, John went about winning at UCLA. Although he was very successful it took him 15 years before he won his first national title. He built the most powerful dynasty in college basketball history, winning 88 straight games and 10 NCAA titles in his last 12 seasons. He was the first man honored in the Basketball Hall of Fame as both a player and coach.

His blueprint for success remains today, as his 15-step Pyramid of Success is a fixture in locker rooms and offices across the nation.

Affirmation: I do the small things that need to be done to be successful.

To think about:

1. Coach Wooden believed the small things counted. List five small things you do that are an example of why you are successful.

2. Coach Wooden is considered a champion coach, but it took him 19 years of college coaching before he won a national championship. How important is laying a foundation? What foundation are you laying for success?

3. Coach Wooden seldom talked about winning, but about giving your best effort. What control do you have over your effort?

Success is a peace of mind, which is a direct result of self-satisfaction in knowing you made the effort to do the best of which you are capable. -John Wooden

Blind and In Prison

John Milton dreamed of being a great poet like one of the greatest figures in literature, William Shakespeare. John was 7 years old at the time Shakespeare died in 1616.

After a promising start early in his education he was expelled for a term from college after starting a fist fight with his tutor. He continued to write, and eventually, his works were published. At the age of 42, he became blind, most likely as a result of untreated glaucoma. But his blindness helped stimulate his verbal richness. In the mid-1650s, Braille had not yet been invented nor had recorded books or any of the technologies that assist visually impaired people today. To go blind in the mid-1650's meant an intellectual death sentence. But John was determined not to let that happen. He dictated his business correspondence to a transcriber for as long as he could, and insisted that his daughters read to him.

Just three months after he lost his eyesight, John's wife Mary died—three days after giving birth to the couple's fourth child. Soon after his wife's death, his 1-year-old son John died as well. John was heartbroken. A few years later, he married his second wife, Katherine. Fifteen months later, Katherine died after giving birth to the couple's only child, who died shortly thereafter.

With his personal life in shambles, John's political fortunes began to decline as well. Involved in a political reformation that fought for civil and religious liberties, the reform failed. He was arrested in 1659 and briefly imprisoned for a few months. After friends intervened to secure his release, he was forced to move out of London and into semi-exile in the country.

The man who dreamed of being a great poet, who went blind and then was imprisoned, did not let those handicaps deter him from developing into a poet whose works were so widely acclaimed he is generally considered the greatest English poet after William Shakespeare.

Affirmation: I persevere through difficult times.

To think about:

1. John's blindness increased his verbal richness. How long would you feel sorry for yourself if you had some of John's challenges? How would you move past them?

2. John's strong beliefs landed him in prison. What are you willing to sacrifice to stand up for what you believe?

3. When John found one road closed, he went down another path. Do you keep your path to success options open?

The mind is its own place and in itself, can make a Heaven of Hell, a Hell of Heaven. -John Milton

Bouncing Back

 There is a rubber tree for every two human beings on earth and the rubber manufacturing business is worth billions of dollars every year. However, the entire process of using rubber may never have existed without a man who refused to give up.

In the 1830's, the rubber manufacturing business became very popular. But a problem was soon discovered; the messy rubber froze hard in winter and turned glue-like in summer. The fledgling rubber companies all went out of business within five years. Rubber was deemed an unfeasible product, and investors lost millions of dollars.

Charles Goodyear, a bankrupt hardware merchant from Philadelphia developed a curiosity with rubber. However, his debt had landed him in jail numerous times. He asked his wife to bring a raw batch of rubber and a rolling pin to his jail cell. Within his cell, he made his first rubber experiments, eventually mixing a dry powder to absorb its stickiness. He made hundreds of pairs of rubber overshoes in his kitchen, but before he could market them, they melted in the summer heat.

He experimented with nitric acid and made a better rubber than anyone had ever made before. But the financial panic of 1837 promptly wiped out his business, ending with his family camped in an abandoned rubber factory on Staten Island, living on fish he caught in the harbor. After five futile years, Goodyear was near rock bottom. He accidently heated his substance one day when it dropped on a stove and to his surprise it altered the rubber into a new substance of weatherproof rubber.

In poor health, he hobbled about conducting his experiments on crutches. At night he lay awake, afraid that he would die and his secret would die with him. He pawned the household furniture, was jailed for nonpayment, and his infant son died. Of the 12 Goodyear children, six died in infancy. Charles died in 1860, $200,000 in debt. Eventually, however, accumulated royalties made his family comfortable. Neither Charles Goodyear nor his family was ever connected with the company named in his honor, today's billion-dollar Goodyear Tire & Rubber Co., the world's largest rubber business.

Affirmation: I bounce back from set-backs.

To think about:

1. Charles Goodyear never gave up despite poor health and financial distress. What are you willing to go through to reach your goal?

2. Charles Goodyear had a vision that was never deterred. What strong is your vision?

3. Although he died deep in debt, Charles Goodyear is now a legend. What will your legacy look like?

A man has cause for regret only when he sows and no one reaps. -Charles Goodyear

Breaking through Barriers

Running a four-minute mile was once deemed impossible. Experts said it was unreachable and dangerous to the health of any athlete who attempted to reach it. Roger Bannister of Great Britain was a 25-year-old medical student at Oxford University completing his internship, putting in long hours at the hospital. His workouts were conducted each day during his 30-minute lunch break. He had been expected to win the 1500 meters at the 1952 Olympics, but Roger was jostled during the race, and never got into contention, finishing fourth.

On May 6, 1954, Roger was scheduled to run at Oxford University's track meet. He had stayed up all night doing his medical rounds and didn't feel like running. But he knew his competitors were closing in on the chase to be the first to run a sub-4:00 mile. He had to go for it! He was paced by a pair of "rabbits," clocking 1:58.2 for the first half-mile. His three-quarter mile time was 3:00.5. With 300 meters to go, Roger said he urged himself "to a supreme effort." He crossed the finish line and began sagging to the ground, drained of all his energy. "It was only then that real pain overtook me," he said. "I felt like an exploded flashlight with no will to live; I just went on existing in the most passive physical state without being unconscious."

The crowd that had urged him on fell silent. Two track officials held him up while spectators converged on him. His time was announced. "Three ... " The rest was drowned out by the cheers. Roger's time of 3:59.4 broke the world record and broke the sub-4:00 barrier, but more importantly, it broke the psychological barrier. What was once deemed impossible had been accomplished. Two years later, 16 runners had logged sub-4:00 miles, accomplishing the one task few thought possible.

Affirmation: I break through barriers.

To think about:

1. Roger Bannister's claim to fame was being the first to break the four-minute mile; however, the true significance was breaking through a barrier. What is the significance behind Roger's achievement?

2. Within two years after Roger Bannister broke the 4:00 barrier, 16 people had broken 4:00. Since then, over 1,300 people have done so. How can something once thought impossible be achieved by so many people?

3. Think about a barrier that limits you. What can you do to break through the barrier?

The man who can drive himself further once the effort gets painful is the man who will win.
-Roger Bannister

Bulb Burns Bright

Thomas Edison was born in 1847 as the seventh and youngest child in his family. In primary school, he lasted only three months as his teacher thought he was mentally inferior, so his mother, who was a school teacher, continued his education at home. He began his lifelong habit of reading and used his talent, intelligence, determination, and a lot of hard work to become one of the greatest success stories in history. He overcame poverty, a physical handicap (after the age of 12, he was virtually deaf) and financial setbacks to become famous and wealthy.

Thomas Edison is considered one of the most prolific inventors in history, holding 1,093 U.S. patents in his name. Among his inventions that had a significant influence on the world, included the phonograph, the motion picture camera, and the electric light bulb. However, not everything Thomas Edison created was a success, he also had some failures.

He formed the Edison Portland Cement Co. in 1899, and made everything from pianos and houses in concrete. Unfortunately, at the time, cement was too expensive and the idea never caught on. Cement wasn't a total failure though, as his company built Yankee Stadium.

When something didn't work the first time, he made a note of exactly what he'd done. Then he adjusted the experiment and tried again. If that failed, he made note, readjusted, and tried again. He kept learning from every experiment. He learned all the ways that it wouldn't work, and each time he found a way that wouldn't work, he knew he was closer to finding a way that would work. It took him approximately 10,000 experiments to invent the electric light bulb. He had to learn by himself, plugging away, failing and learning, until he finally worked out the right way to do it.

In 1914, Thomas Edison's factory in New Jersey was virtually destroyed by fire. Although the damage exceeded $2 million, the buildings were insured for only $238,000 because they were made of concrete and were thought to be fireproof. Much of his life work went up in flames that night. The next morning, Edison looked at the ruins and said, "There is great value in disaster. All our mistakes are burned up. Thank God we can start anew."

Affirmation: I learn from my mistakes and become better.

To think about:

1. Thomas Edison was not afraid to fail. In fact, his failures set the stage for his success. Think of times your failure has contributed to your eventual success.

2. How do you react to failure?

3. What can you learn from the attitude of Edison?

Many of life's failures are men who did not realize how close they were to success when they gave up. -Thomas Edison

Composing a Masterpiece

Considered by many experts as the greatest musician of all time, Ludwig van Beethoven, was born the eldest of three children. At a young age he became interested in music and was taught by his father. His father was determined Ludwig would be a famous musician and used extraordinary means that affected Ludwig the rest of his life. His father would beat him for each hesitation or mistake. On a near daily basis, Beethoven was flogged, locked in the cellar and deprived of sleep in order to practice for a few extra hours. Whether in spite of or because of his father's methods, Ludwig was a prodigiously talented musician from his earliest days.

At the age of 7, the child prodigy gave his first public performance. Before he was 12, he published his first work and began to study with the greatest musicians of his time. In 1801, at the age of 31, Ludwig started to go deaf. He wrote a famous text expressing his disgust at the unfairness of life: that he, a musician, could become deaf was something he did not want to live through. However, his passion for music motivated him to carry on and he wrote that he knew that he still had many other musical domains to explore.

By the last decade of his life he was almost totally deaf. Knowing that his handicap was getting worse and worse, he gave up conducting and performing in public but he focused on creating great music, writing an opera and some overtures, and composed many symphonies. His most admired works came from this period when he was almost totally deaf and could not hear his own music.

Ludwig van Beethoven is widely considered the greatest composer of all time. The fact he composed his best music while deaf is an almost superhuman feat of creative genius.

I will seize fate by the throat; it shall certainly never wholly overcome me. -Ludwig van Beethoven

Crazy Horse

Sculptor Korczak Ziolkowski believed that nothing was impossible as long as you were willing to work hard enough and pay the price. Born in Boston, Massachusetts, of Polish parents in 1908, he persevered through a difficult childhood. He was orphaned when he was only 1 year old and placed in multiple foster homes, where he was badly mistreated. Through the difficult childhood, Korcazk learned to work hard as he acquired heavy construction skills helping his foster father. His difficult life prepared him to prevail over decades of financial hardship and racial prejudice he encountered trying to create an American Indian memorial in the Black Hills.

Although he had never take a lesson in art or sculpturing, he studied the experts and started a successful studio career doing commissioned sculpture. In 1939, he was asked to assist Buzon Borglum in creating the sculptures at Mount Rushmore. It was there he met Lakota Chief Henry Standing Bear, who asked him to create a memorial to American Indians. After serving his country in World War II, he turned down invitations to create war memorials in Europe and dedicated his life to creating the Crazy Horse Memorial to the American Indian people.

He would spend the rest of his life on the mountain, nearly 36 years of hard, daily work, without taking any salary. Korczak believed in the "if it is to be it is up to me," philosophy. He did find the time to get married, and Korczak and his wife had 10 children whom he schooled in the special skills of mountain carving.

When Korczak died at the age of 74, he passed the torch, leaving the dream of building the Crazy Horse Monument to his family. Seven of his children remained to work on the project.

When completed, the Crazy Horse mountain carving will be the largest carving in the world, at 641 feet long by 563 feet high, a few feet taller than the Washington Monument, and many times the size of nearby Mount Rushmore.

Affirmation: I follow my dreams.

To think about:

1. Korczak dedicated his life to a monumental task. The Crazy Horse monument, when completed, will be his legacy. What might your legacy be?

2. Korczak spent nearly every day on the mountain in a labor of love. What is your labor of love?

3. Korczak kept his promise to the Indian people to build a monument. How long does a promise last?

A very great vision is needed and the man who has it must follow it as the eagle seeks the deepest blue of the sky. -Crazy Horse, Sioux Chief

Desire to Serve

Born in Russia as Golda Mabovitz, Golda Meir came to the United States at the age of 8. Golda grew up in Milwaukee, Wisconsin. Her childhood was marked by cold, hunger, and poverty that claimed the lives of five siblings, and the memory of her father boarding the family's front door in response to threats against Jews.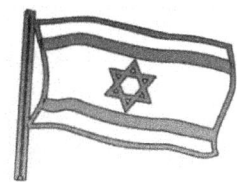

Golda and her husband moved to Palestine and she worked as a teacher before moving up in the political ranks. Golda became involved in the Zionist movement and took part in the creation of the state of Israel after World War II.

Golda worked for the Israeli government in various roles including as its minister to Moscow. At the age of 71, she became Prime Minister of the State of Israel in March, 1969. The world's third woman to be head of state of a country (after Sri Lanka and India), she was strong-willed, with remarkable strength.

As Prime Minister of Israel, she presided over the country during the rescue of hostages at Entebbe and the turn-around during the Yom Kippur war. Meir's legacy is one of complete commitment to the Jewish people.

Golda Meir was one of the founders of Israel and the most prominent woman politician of her era. She overcame many personal hardships because she was a woman. Golda possessed a rare mixture of courage and sincerity. She achieved fame through hard work and was admired for her simplicity and straight talk. All her life she simply set out to do a job, whatever that might be, and poured into it every ounce of energy and dedication she could summon. Her aspiration to lead arose not for the lure of power, but through a desire to serve.

Affirmation: I serve others.

To think about:

1. Golda poured all her energy into getting the job done. Can you say you pour all your energy into what you do?

2. Do you have a desire to serve? How can you help others?

3. What inner spark could you develop into a flame of achievement?

Trust yourself. Create the kind of self that you will be happy to live with all your life. Make the most of yourself by fanning the tiny, inner sparks of possibility into flames of achievement.
-Golda Meir

Determination

 In 1883, a creative engineer named John Roebling was inspired by an idea to build a spectacular bridge connecting Manhattan and Brooklyn. However, bridge building experts throughout the world thought that this was an impossible feat and told him to forget the idea. It just could not be done. It was not practical. It had never been done before.

John could not ignore the vision he had in his mind of this bridge. After much discussion and persuasion, he managed to convince his son Washington, an up and coming engineer, that the bridge could be built. The father and son developed concepts of how it could be accomplished and how the obstacles could be overcome. With great excitement over the challenge ahead of them, they hired their crew and began to build their dream bridge.

Only a few months into construction, a tragic accident on the site took the life of John Roebling. His son Washington was injured, left with brain damage, and unable to move or talk.

Since the Roeblings were the only ones who knew how the bridge could be built, people felt that the project should be stopped. In spite of his handicap, Washington's mind was still sharp and he still had a burning desire to complete the bridge. Suddenly an idea hit him. All he could do was move one finger, so he slowly developed a code of communication with his wife by touching her arm with that one finger. For 13 years, Washington tapped out his instructions with his finger on his wife's arm, until the bridge was finally completed. Today, the spectacular Brooklyn Bridge stands as a glorious tribute to the triumph of one man's indomitable spirit and his determination not to be defeated by circumstances.

When we face obstacles in our day-to-day life, our hurdles seem very small in comparison to what many others have to face. The Brooklyn Bridge shows us that dreams that seem impossible can be realized with determination and persistence, no matter the odds.

Affirmation: My determination makes me successful.

To think about:

1. What goal have you had that has taken you the longest to achieve?

2. When obstacles appear in your path to success, what are some specific steps you could do to overcome them?

3. Do you know someone who has overcome adversity to be successful? What are some of their traits that have made them successful?

One man has enthusiasm for 30 minutes, another for 30 days, but it is the man who has it for 30 years who makes a success of his life. -Edward B. Butler

Dream for a World of Hope

Terry Fox was an active teenager, successfully involved in numerous sports. When he was 18, he was diagnosed with bone cancer, which forced him to have his right leg amputated above the knee in 1977. The night before his amputation, he read about an amputee runner and dreamed of  running after his surgery. While in the hospital, he became emotionally connected to the suffering of the other patients, most of them being children. In order to raise money and awareness for cancer research, he had a dream of running across Canada. His run was called the Marathon of Hope. Running in his distinctive run-hop style, he ran approximately 26 miles a day. As he started his way across Canada, crowds showed up to watch him run, and despite sores and abrasions under his prosthetics, he kept running. He ran 3,339 miles in 143 days when he was forced to stop running outside of Thunder Bay, Ontario, because cancer had appeared in his lungs.

Terry's hope of raising an amount of money equaling one dollar for every Canadian to fight cancer was realized. In 1981, the Canadian national population reached 24.1 million and the Terry Fox Marathon of Hope Fund totaled 24.17 million dollars. The Marathon of Hope dream had come true. The following year, Terry passed away at the age of 22.

Terry Fox's courage has not been forgotten. Mount Terry Fox, a peak in the Rocky Mountains is a lasting symbol of his courage. A portion of the Trans-Canada Highway was renamed the Terry Fox Courage Highway. Terry was inducted posthumously into the Canadian Sports Hall of Fame. He was also honored on a Canadian coin and postage stamp.

Terry Fox was the boy who never gave up. His short life was devoted to achieving his goals. Obstacles just made him try harder. When he learned he had cancer and would lose his leg, he resolved to do something to help other cancer victims. He has left a legacy of hope that has inspired millions to continue his cause.

Affirmations: I overcome obstacles.

To think about:

1. Terry did not feel sorry for himself and made a commitment to help raise cancer awareness. How do you avoid feeling sorry for yourself?

2. Terry displayed tremendous courage. How do you define courage?

3. How do you display courage?

I'm not a dreamer, and I'm not saying this will initiate any kind of definitive answer or cure to cancer, but I believe in miracles. I have to. -Terry Fox

Father's Love

When Rick Hoyt was born, the umbilical cord wrapped around his neck at birth, depriving his brain of oxygen. He was diagnosed as a quadriplegic with cerebral palsy. The doctors said it would be impossible for him to lead a normal life and he should be placed in an institution. However, his parents had other plans. Rick's parents tried to raise him like any other child. Originally, Rick had no means to communicate, until an interactive computer allowed Rick to select highlighted letters with the tap of his head. Rick was finally accepted into public school at the age of 13.

One day, Rick wanted to enter a five-mile charity run. His dad had no running background, but he did have a tremendous work ethic. He had grown up chopping wood to heat the family house which was without running water or an indoor bathroom. So, Dick pushed Rick in his heavy wheelchair through the five-mile race, finishing next to last. Dick was in agony after the race, but the pain went away when Rick typed out the message, "Dad, when I'm running, it feels like I'm not handicapped." That was the beginning of team Hoyt.

The sense of sacrifice created by the intense bond between the two increased as they began to race each weekend. Their clumsy wheelchair was replaced by a custom-made chair with lightweight tubes and tires. Team Hoyt started running marathons and became the face of the Boston Marathon, as there is a statue of them both near the starting line. Team Hoyt has completed more than 1,000 distance races and triathlons, including six Ironman competitions. They also biked and ran across America in 1992, covering 3,735 miles from Los Angeles to Boston in 45 consecutive days.

Rick achieved a tremendous milestone in graduating from Boston University after persevering for nine years to earn his degree in special education. With the mantra of "yes you can," the Hoyts created the Hoyt Foundation to help America's disabled youth integrate into society and take up endurance events.

Affirmation: Yes you can.

To think about:

1. The Hoyt's bonded together as a team. How does working closely with someone create a bonding?

2. Dick Hoyt's love for his son motivated him to accomplish great tasks. How does your love for something motivate you?

3. On days you feel sorry for yourself, how can the Team Hoyt story motivate you?

When we first started running, I was getting calls and letters from people with disabilities that were very upset with me and they said I was just out there looking for glory and dragging my disabled son to all these races. They didn't know that it was him dragging his old man to these races. -Dick Hoyt

Find A Way

Diana Nyad was 8 years old when she first dreamed about swimming across the 100 plus mile Straits of Florida. Eventually Diana became a swimming sensation, winning multiple swimming marathons, and she was one of the first women to swim around the island of Manhattan. In her first attempt to cross the Straits of Florida in 1978, rough seas left her battered, delirious and less than halfway toward her goal. She tried to accomplish the feat three more times. All four tries were marked by gut-wrenching setbacks. The seas were rough and drained her energy. She would fight hour-long asthma attacks, or the jellyfish stings would leave her with excruciating pain. She moved on with life, but the dream lived on.

Thirty-five years after her first attempt, she would try again at age 64. She was determined to "find a way." She jumped into the ocean in Havana, Cuba, to begin her fifth try in 35 years. The wind was strong, and she was taking in salt water, becoming nauseous, vomiting, and shivering. She never imagined she would suffer so much. Through it all, she kept repeating her mantra, "find a way."

Swimming 53 hours in the water, she willed her way to a Key West beach, becoming the first person to swim from Cuba to Florida without a protective cage. Her face was sunburned and swollen, but her accomplishment was monumental. Her message (after getting out of the water, her speech was slurred because of a swollen tongue and lips) is one that tells us we should never, ever give up and that you are never too old to chase your dreams.

Affirmation: I will find a way.

To think about:

1. Diana Nyad never gave up on her dream. Do you have dreams you are committed to for a lifetime?

2. How could the mantra, "find a way," help you to achieve goals?

3. How does Diana's feat compare to the toughest feat you have accomplished?

The spirit is larger than the body. The body is pathetic compared to what we have inside us.
-Diana Nyad

Gazelle

Wilma Rudolph's race in life started very slowly as the 20th of 22 children. She was born prematurely and weighed only 4.5 pounds at birth. Because of racial segregation, Wilma and her mother could not receive medical care at the local hospital because it was for whites only. The only black doctor was 50 miles away, which was a hardship on the Rudolph family's budget. Through the next several years, Wilma faced one hardship after another in the form of measles, mumps, scarlet fever, chicken pox, and double pneumonia.

When Wilma was 6 years old, it was discovered that her left leg and foot were becoming weak and deformed with polio, a crippling disease that had no cure. The doctor told Wilma that she would never walk again. Wilma and her mother were determined not to give up. With the help of the black medical college of Fisk University in Nashville, Wilma went through vigorous physical therapy using crutches, braces, and corrective shoes. Finally, by the age of 12, she could walk normally and decided to become an athlete.

In high school, Wilma became a basketball star, setting state records for scoring and leading her team to the state championship. By the time she was 16, she earned a berth on the U.S. Olympic track and field team and came home from the 1956 Melbourne Games with an Olympic bronze medal in the 4x100-meter relay.

At the 1960 Summer Olympics in Rome, 80,000 spectators filled the Olympic Stadium in temperatures hotter than 100 degrees. In the 100 meters, she tied the world record of 11.3 seconds in the semifinals, and then won the final in 11.0. In the 200 meters, she broke the Olympic record in the opening heat in 23.2 and won the final in 24.0. In the 4x100-meter relay, Wilma, despite a poor baton pass, overtook Germany's anchor leg and the Americans, all women from Tennessee State, took the gold in 44.5 after setting a world record of 44.4 in the semifinals.

Wilma did more than promote her country. In her soft-spoken, gracious manner, she paved the way for future African American athletes, both men and women.

Affirmation: I am fulfilling my potential for greatness.

To think about:

1. Wilma Rudolph could not walk normally until she was 12, yet four years later, she was on the Olympic team. Do you ever think something is impossible?

2. Wilma was gracious and humble as an athlete. On a scale of 1-10 (10 being high), how humble are you?

3. How does the Wilma Rudolph story inspire you?

Never underestimate the power of dreams and the influence of the human spirit. We are all the same in this notion: The potential for greatness lives within each of us. -Wilma Rudolph

Golden Arches

Ray Kroc looked for success for a long time. In his first 57 years of life, he made a good living but was never a great success. However, he was always ready for an opportunity. He sold malt mixers and he had an account with the McDonald brothers, who owned a small hamburger stand in California. The McDonald bothers wanted to make lots of malts at the same time. Ray saw the potential in the restaurant and encouraged the brothers to make it into a franchise. Ray  pitched his vision of creating McDonald's restaurants all over the U.S. to the brothers. Ray stayed persistent and kept hounding the brothers until they agreed to allow him to sell franchises. In 1955, he founded the McDonald's Corporation, and five years later, he bought the exclusive rights to the McDonald's name. By 1958, McDonald's had sold its 100 millionth hamburger.

In the first six years, Ray sold 200 McDonald's franchises. Eventually it would develop into a billion dollar company. Why did McDonald's strike success and become the most well-known fast food franchise in history? The menu is brief; containing only items whose consistent quality can be maintained in thousands of stores. There are strict standards for service, cleanliness, and store operations and the company is constantly researching the market to determine what consumers want and then creating an effective advertising message.

Ray Kroc was well over the age of 50 when he realized the American dream. Although he knew there would be problems and temporary failures, he moved forward and with his hard work, he established the most successful restaurant chain in history. From his passion for innovation and efficiency, to his relentless pursuit of quality, and his many charitable contributions, Ray Kroc created an inspirational legacy.

Affirmation: I relentlessly pursue quality.

To think about:

1. Part of McDonald's success its efficiency. Do you work efficiently?

2. Ray Kroc found success late in life. Are you willing to forego instant gratification for long-term success?

3. Ray Kroc relentlessly pursued quality. What does the term "relentless pursuit of quality" mean to you?

Luck is a dividend of sweat. The more you sweat, the luckier you get. -Ray Kroc

Hard Work Reaps Rewards

Ewing Kauffman enjoyed sports as a youth. He liked the challenges that sports provided and received much satisfaction in putting a great effort into them. His sports career came to an end at the age of 11, as he was struck with a severe illness that left him with a faulty heart valve. The doctor prescribed a year of bedrest. Ewing had to lay flat on his back, and he couldn't even sit-up or leave his bed for an entire year! But Ewing didn't waste his time.

He began reading books and read over 100 books a month. He read the Bible several times, and he read adventure books and books on medicine, math, and astronomy.

After his recovery, he finished school and joined the Navy. Following World War II, Ewing began working as a salesman for a pharmaceutical company. In 1950, his entrepreneurial spirit led him to start his own pharmaceutical company in the basement of his home. He packaged vitamin pills at night and sold them during the day.

He named his company Marion Laboratories Inc., using his middle name rather than his last name so his customers wouldn't perceive him as a one-man operation. He brought major league baseball back to his hometown when he bought the Kansas City Royals, boosting civic pride and the city's economy. With the same entrepreneurial vision he used in business, he made the Royals a model sports franchise. The team developed young players who won six division titles, two American League pennants, and a World Series championship in 1985.

Ewing Kauffman turned the misfortune of an illness into an opportunity to better himself. He used three major principles to guide his successful life.

- Treat others as you want to be treated
- Share life's rewards with those who make them possible
- Give back to society

Affirmation: I treat others the way I would want to be treated.

To think about:

1. When Ewing lay flat on his back for a year, he didn't feel sorry for himself, he used that as an opportunity to get better. How can you turn a possible excuse into an opportunity?

2. Ewing gave back to society. What will you give back to society?

3. Rate yourself on a scale of 1-10 (1 low, 10 high) on how you are treating others as you want to be treated.

Those who apply themselves unswervingly to a task are amply rewarded. -Ewing M. Kauffman

Helping Through Medical Discoveries

Growing up, Louis Pasteur was just an average student making average grades in school. Despite the average grades, he worked hard to become a teacher, and he eventually became a professor of chemistry at the University of Strasbourg in France.

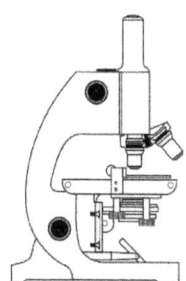

Married, he had five children with three of them dying in childhood of typhoid fever. That may have been one of the factors that led Louis to dedicate his life to save people from disease.

He discovered microbes were responsible for souring alcohol and came up with a process where bacteria is destroyed by heating beverages and then allowing them to cool. This process was named after him—pasteurization.

Louis Pasteur was partially paralyzed in 1868 due to a severe brain stroke, but still continued his research. His first vaccine discovery was in 1879, with a disease called chicken cholera. His various investigations convinced him that germs attack the body from the outside. Many felt that tiny organisms such as germs could not possibly kill larger ones such as humans. Louis fought to convince surgeons that germs existed and carried diseases, and dirty instruments and hands spread germs, and therefore, disease. His pasteurization process killed germs and prevented the spread of disease. He went on to extend his germ theory to develop causes and vaccinations for diseases such as anthrax, cholera, tuberculosis, smallpox, and rabies.

From his beginnings as a very average student to overcoming the challenges of a stroke later in life, Louis Pasteur was one of the most important founders of medical microbiology. He is remembered for his remarkable breakthroughs in the causes and preventions of diseases.

Affirmation: I help other people.

To think about:

1. Louis stated that chance favors the prepared mind. What does that mean to you?

2. Many experts felt that Louis's theories were wrong, but he continued to work on what he believed in. How strong is your faith when others doubt your action?

3. Louis dedicated his life to helping others. Is your focus only on yourself or on others?

Did you ever observe to whom the accidents happen? Chance favors only the prepared mind.
-Louis Pasteur

Let me tell you the secret that has led me to my goal. My strength lies solely in my tenacity.
-Louis Pasteur

I am an Alcoholic

 Bill Wilson had his first drink in the Army and soon started drinking heavily. He became a successful stock trader on Wall Street but lost all his money in the stock market crash of 1929. His drinking became heavier and heavier, and it started to take over his life. Finally, hitting rock bottom, he spent most of his days and nights in a drunken stupor.

Bill was committed to a hospital for drug and alcohol addictions four different times. The prevailing theory at the time was that alcoholism was a matter of both physical and mental control. Bill gained hope from his doctor's assertion that alcoholism was a medical condition rather than a moral failing, but even that knowledge could not help him. He was eventually told that he would either die from his alcoholism or have to be locked up permanently.

Eventually, Bill had a spiritual awakening and a belief that God would help him overcome his addiction to alcohol. He realized that he couldn't do it alone. During a business trip, he was tempted to drink again and decided that to remain sober, he needed to help another alcoholic. He found another alcoholic named Dr. Robert Smith and they soon began to hold meetings for recovering alcoholics who were looking for help. They became the founders of what would later become known as Alcoholics Anonymous.

When the group had about 100 members, Bill began to write down his philosophy as a series of principles for remaining sober. Bill felt that the key to sobriety was a change of heart. He defined 12 steps to recovery that included an admission that one is powerless over the addiction, a belief in a higher power, making restitution for the wrong one has committed, and service to others. Today, Alcoholics Anonymous (A.A.) has more than two million members in over 150 countries. A.A.'s success in helping alcoholics caused the America Medical Association to officially recognize alcoholism as a disease instead of a failure of will power in 1956.

Bill Wilson recognized his shortcomings and was able to take his own flaws and apply them so other people would recognize them within themselves. Never interested in making money, but only in helping others, he sacrificed his personal life and wants and needs. His positive influence on others was reflected in being selected one of Time magazine's "100 Persons of the Century."

Affirmation: I will make a difference.

To think about:

1. Alcoholics Anonymous is successful because of the support the members give each other. How do you contribute to making a group successful?

2. Think of three examples where you helped others and felt good after you did so.

3. What are three ways you could help somebody in the next week?

To the world you may be one person, but to one person you may be the world. -Bill Wilson

I Can Do Something

Helen Keller started life just like any other child born with two major senses, sight and hearing. She started speaking at six months old and walking at the age of 1. However, after the age of 1, she contracted an illness that produces a high body temperature. Helen had the fever a couple of days, and when it went away, she had lost her sight and hearing at just 18 months old.

Helen's parents were determined to find help for their daughter. Many family members felt Helen should be institutionalized, as she would often go into raging tantrums. Eventually, her parents found the Perkins Institute for the Blind where Helen began to work with Anne Sullivan, a former graduate of the institute. Anne displayed an amazing dedication as Helen's teacher, and their relationship lasted an amazing 49 years.

Anne first started teaching Helen finger spelling. Helen's frustrations grew and her tantrums increased before she finally made a connection between the object and the letters when she dipped her hand in water to understand the word, "water." Helen would toil for 25 years to learn to speak so others could understand her.

With her teacher, Anne Sullivan, by her side, Helen attended college and graduated with honors. Through her many speeches and appearances, she brought inspiration and encouragement to millions of people. In 1920, Helen helped found the American Civil Liberties Union. During her lifetime, she received many honors in recognition of her accomplishments.

Helen Keller's remarkable life stands as a powerful example of how determination, hard work, and imagination can allow an individual to triumph over adversity. With a great deal of persistence, she overcame difficult conditions and grew into a respected and world-renowned activist who labored for the betterment of others.

Affirmation: I am determined.

To think about:

1. How do your struggles compare with what Helen went through?

2. Helen had an outstanding mentor in Anne Sullivan. Who has served as a mentor for you?

3. How could you serve as mentor for someone?

The best and most beautiful things in the world cannot be seen or even touched - they must be felt with the heart. -Helen Keller

I am only one, but still I am one. I cannot do everything, but still I can do something; and because I cannot do everything, I will not refuse to do something that I can do.
-Helen Keller

I Have a Dream

Born as Michael King, Jr. on January, 15, 1929, his name was later changed to Martin Luther King. His parents tried to shield him from racism as he was growing up. His father fought against racial prejudice, not just because his race suffered, but because he considered racism and segregation to be an affront to God's will. His father strongly discouraged any sense of class superiority in his children, which left a lasting impression on young Michael.

Michael skipped both the ninth and eleventh grades and entered Morehouse College in Atlanta at age 15. As a student, he was unmotivated the first two years and questioned religion in general, feeling uncomfortable with overly emotional displays of religious worship. This discomfort continued through much of his adolescence.

On the night that Rosa Parks was arrested for refusing to give up her bus seat, Michael and other local civil rights leaders lead a city-wide bus boycott. Michael was elected to lead the boycott because he was young, well-trained with solid family connections and had professional standing. But he was also new to the community and had few enemies, so it was felt he would have strong credibility within the black community.

Martin led the civil rights demonstrations. He organized a demonstration in downtown Birmingham, Alabama, where entire families attended. City police turned dogs and fire hoses on demonstrators and Martin was jailed, along with a large number of his supporters, but the event drew national attention. On August, 28, 1961, the historic March on Washington drew more than 200,000 people in the shadow of the Lincoln Memorial. It was here that he made his famous "I Have a Dream" speech; emphasizing his belief that someday all men could be brothers.

Martin Luther King, Jr.'s life had a huge impact on race relations in the United States. Years after his death, he is the most widely known African-American leader of his era. His life and work have been honored with a national holiday, schools, and public buildings named after him, and a memorial in Washington, D.C.

Affirmation: I have a dream.

To think about:

1. Dr. King had a vision of what America could look like. What vision do you have of your future life?

2. What steps will you need to achieve in order to accomplish your vision?

3. Martin Luther King, Jr. was a leader. In what ways do you lead?

Faith is taking the first step even when you don't see the whole staircase. -Martin Luther King, Jr.

Imagination Runs Wild

Theodore Geisel had an imagination that ran wild. He had a gift for inventing words and making them rhyme and creating interesting kinds of characters. He wrote his first book for children and had high hopes of persuading a publishing company to print it. He knocked on the door to present his manuscript and the publishing company rejected it. Theodore was not discouraged and went to a second publishing company. The same thing happened; it was rejected again. He went to another publisher, and another, and another. They all said no!

Theodore did not give up, even after 23 rejections. He went to number 24 and they said "yes!" That book sold over six million copies. Geisel went on to write more than 50 books that have sold more than 200 million copies in 17 different languages.

Would you have given up after the first rejection, the third rejection, or even the 10th? Would you have knocked on over 20 doors before giving up?

Theodore Geisel's story is an example of staying positive, even when things don't go your way. We all start out in a positive frame of mind, but after a few failures, that positive attitude begins to drain out of us.

You may have read some of Theodore Geisel's books such as *Green Eggs and Ham* and *The Cat in the Hat*. You see, Theodore Geisel's pen name was Dr. Seuss, one of the most beloved children's writers in history.

Affirmation: I am committed to staying positive.

To think about:

1. What do you focus on when you feel rejected?

2. How do you continue to pursue your dreams even through failure?

3. Life has a way of being a self-fulfilling prophecy. If you always expect the worst, then you will never be disappointed. If you expect the best, that sets the stage for positive things to happen. How do you expect the best, even under challenging situations?

Let us not become weary in doing good, for at the proper time we will reap a harvest if we do not give up. -Galatians 6:9

Iron Man

Photo courtesy of Kansas Athletics

When he was 7 years old, Glenn and his older brother Floyd had the chore of starting a fire in the rural schoolhouse stove every cold morning. One February morning in 1916, the kerosene container had accidentally been filled with gasoline. The stove exploded and both Glenn and Floyd were terribly burned. There was no phone and no ambulance, so they ran two miles home before receiving treatment. Floyd died, and Glenn's legs were so badly burned that his doctors told him he would never walk again. He was bed-ridden for months. Showing a fierce determination and with a great deal of agony, he slowly began to recover and was able to walk on crutches. Finally, he got rid of the crutches but, as he said later, "It hurt like thunder to walk, but it didn't hurt at all when I ran. So for five or six years, about all I did was run."

Glenn became a miler in high school in Elkhart, Kansas, and set a national high school record of 4:24.7 in his last race. He entered the University of Kansas in 1931 and won the NCAA 1500-meter title in 1932. Glenn went on to finish fourth in the 1932 Olympic 1500 meters. In the 1936 Olympic Games in Berlin, he put on a burst of speed in the third lap to try to break away from the field, but took a silver medal behind New Zealand's Jack Lovelock, who ran a world record time of 3:47.8.

Because of circulation problems caused by his childhood accident, Glenn needed nearly an hour to prepare for a race. He first had to massage his legs and he then required a long warm-up period. He overcame the odds and was the fastest American miler during the 1930s, setting a world record in 1934 of 4:06.8, and also an 800-meter world record of 1:49.7.

Affirmation: I am determined.

To think about:

1. How did Glenn Cunningham overcome his adversity?

2. Think of an adversity that you have had. How did you overcome it?

3. What do you think is the most important factor in overcoming a challenge?

For in running it is man against himself, the cruelest of opponents. The other runners are not the real enemies. His adversary lies within him, in his ability, with brain and heart to master himself and his emotions. -Glenn Cunningham

I Will Do My Best

James West had a challenging childhood. His father died around the time of his birth, and his mother was hospitalized when he was young and James was placed in an orphanage. By the age of 10, he was crippled, with one leg being shorter than the other. He would be challenged by this handicap for the rest of his life. Despite being 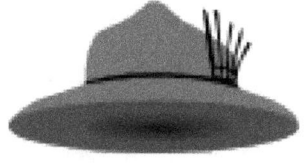 physically disabled, James drove himself through high school with a fierce determination, persevering to become a successful attorney.

James believed that youth should have opportunities and was a strong advocate for those opportunities. He became the first Chief Scout Executive of the Boys Scouts of America (BSA), serving as their leader for 32 years, becoming one of the most important figures in the history of the Boy Scout movement. His fierce determination created the organization and provided the momentum to help build Scouting into one of the largest and most effective youth organizations in the world.

Today, the Boy Scouts of America is one of the largest youth organizations in the United States, with 2.7 million youth members and over one million adult volunteers. Since its founding in 1910 as part of the international Scout movement, more than 110 million Americans have been members of the Boy Scouts of America.

The goal of the Boy Scouts is to train youth in responsible citizenship, character development, and self-reliance through participation in a wide range of activities. It instills in youth the typical Scouting values such as trustworthiness, good citizenship, and outdoors skills.

James West's challenging childhood kindled a fire that led to a raging inferno that has helped millions of youth to develop lifelong skills to become productive citizens.

Affirmation: I have a fierce determination.

To think about:

1. How did James West's challenging childhood set the stage for him to devote his life to opportunities for youth?

2. James determination helped him survive a difficult childhood and led to adult success. How will what you establish now, help you down the road in the future?

3. A goal of the Boy Scouts is to develop character. How is character developed?

The only disability in life is a bad attitude. -Scott Hamilton

Keeping the Faith

Joane was struggling to make ends meet. Her mother had recently died, she was recently divorced with a small child, and she was living on welfare. While she was traveling on a train, she had an idea for a book and started to write. Once she had completed the book, she submitted it to numerous publishers but was rejected time after time. Finally, she was able to find a publisher for the book and the book sold very well. The publisher had such success with the book; Joane wrote two more books for the series. In fact, the three books climbed into the top three positions on the New York Times best-seller list. Those three books earned $489 million in three years, with over 35 million copies sold in 35 different languages. Another book followed, and became the fastest selling book in history. A fifth, sixth, and seventh book followed in the series.

From living in poverty and on welfare, Joane catapulted to Britain's 12th wealthiest woman, even wealthier than the queen. Her books have sold over 400 million copies, becoming the best-selling book series in history, and have been turned into movies, smashing box office records.

Who was this rags to riches story? You may have read her books or seen the movies. Anticipating that the target audience of young boys might not want to read a book written by a woman, her publishers demanded that she use two initials, rather than her full name. As she had no middle name, she chose K as the second initial of her pen name, from her paternal grandmother.

You may know her as J.K. Rowling. If the name doesn't sound familiar, perhaps you've heard of Harry Potter. J.K. Rowling, the creator of the Harry Potter series, who kept the faith in her ability as a writer, became one of the most successful authors of all-time.

Affirmation: I keep the faith.

To think about:

1. Joane kept the faith in her writing ability. What does it mean to keep the faith?

2. Joane was rejected many times by publishers. Does rejection discourage or motivate you?

3. How can you use failure as a learning experience?

Never trust anything that can think for itself if you can't see where it keeps its brain.
-J.K. Rowling

Keep on Knocking

When Harland retired at the age of 65, he had little to show for a life's work and only had a $105 monthly pension check to live on. Knowing he did not have enough money to live off of, he decided to try and sell his chicken recipe. His plan was to sell his recipe to restaurant owners, who would in turn give him 5 cents for every piece of chicken sold. The first restaurant owner he called on turned him down.

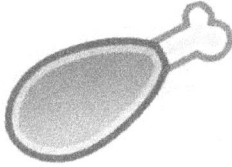

So did the second and the third. The first 1,000 restaurants Harland went to turned him down, but he continued to call on owners as he traveled across the United States, sleeping in his car to save money.

Finally, the 1,009th restaurant said "yes!" He continued to call on restaurants for the next two years but only signed up a total of five restaurants. Still, Harland did not get discouraged. He knew he had a great chicken recipe and believed his idea would catch on.

Earlier in his life, Harland was involved in other business ventures; but they weren't successful. He had a gas station in the 30s, a restaurant in the 40s, and he gave up on both of them.

At the age of 65, however, Harland "Colonel" Sanders decided his Kentucky Fried Chicken idea was the right idea, and he refused to give up, even in spite of repeated rejection. His idea finally caught on. Now, hundreds of Kentucky Fried Chicken restaurants all across the country sell his secret recipe with 11 herbs and spices, making Harland a multi-millionaire.

Affirmation: I am persistent.

To think about:

1. If you feel like giving up on something, what extra effort are you willing to put into it to be successful?

2. Harland Sanders was passionate about his chicken recipe. What are you passionate about?

3. How can you use that passion to be a success?

Be persistent. Never give up. Keep on knocking. Keep on asking. Keep on seeking.

Kiss of Kindness

Milton Hershey's father moved from place to place investing in numerous businesses that failed. His son Milton attended seven schools in eight years and never made it past the fourth grade. With a lack of education, Milton first worked as a printer, but was fired. That led him to being an apprentice to a candy maker. After serving his apprenticeship, he opened up his own candy store in Philadelphia, but it failed. Undeterred, he moved to Denver to open another candy shop. That also failed. He moved to New York City to open another shop. That, too, failed.

Frustrated, but still determined, he returned to his hometown in Pennsylvania and began making caramels. That business prospered, and Milton built a factory on his store site. In 1893, he was inspired by German chocolate makers at the World's Fair and began to produce his own chocolate.

The Hershey Chocolate Company quickly became successful. His factory became the largest chocolate factory in the world. As the company grew and Hershey's wealth expanded, so did his vision for creating a model community. In the town that came to be known as Hershey, Pennsylvania, Hershey built schools, parks, churches, recreational facilities, and housing for his employees. Unable to have children of their own, the Hersheys focused a good portion of their giving on endeavors dedicated to children.

While he seldom wrote or read, and had been forced to leave school early after the fourth grade, Milton was driven to make sure those around him received a great education.

Affirmation: I make others feel good.

To think about:

1. Milton Hershey gave to his community. What do you give to your community?

2. Despite early failures, Milton kept on trying. What do you learn from your failures?

3. Milton believed that an education was important and encouraged others to become educated. How will an education enhance your opportunities?

One is only happy in proportion as he makes others feel happy and only useful as he contributes his influences for the finer callings in life. -Milton Hershey

Laughed at His Paper

Allen Neuharth's father died when he was 2, and he learned to be independent while he was growing up. He became the newspaper editor of his high school paper and at the University of South Dakota.

As a teenager, he gave up sports and extracurricular activities and focused on how he could make money. He raised $50,000 from friends and relatives to start a paper, a weekly tabloid called "SoDak Sports." It was a well-written, informative paper, filled with statistics, and it was also innovative, as it carried results of women's sports when no one else was. However, after two years, it folded and Allen was left broke and discouraged.

In the next 25 years, Allen worked his way up in the newspaper industry to manage Gannett Papers. Gannett Papers was mostly a chain of small-town, bland newspapers, devoting more space to church suppers than to in-depth reporting. Although Gannett Papers grew under Allen, it bothered him that it had a reputation for mediocrity, as it had no papers in any major markets.

Finally, Allen decided he would take all the lessons he had learned working on small town papers and apply them to a national paper. He felt there were millions of potential readers with neither the time nor the inclination to read the kind of newspapers that already existed. He wanted a paper with a jazzy display of color and graphics; charts filled with facts; tidbits about small-town America; upbeat stories about people, articles about TV, film, and rock personalities; and lots of sports with statistics; and a comprehensive weather map, with most of the stories in less than 500 words.

Critics said it would never work. The paper lost millions and millions of dollars, but Allen never gave up on his idea. Eventually, it started to get into the black with Allen, as chairman of the Gannett Company. Triumphantly, overcoming the odds, Allen Neuharth turned a small-town newspaper into "The Nation's Newspaper." Today his paper—**USA TODAY**—is read by more people (5.5 million) than any other newspaper in the country.

Affirmation: I believe in myself.

To think about:

1. Allen Neuharth refused to give up on his dream. What dreams do you have that you are willing to invest time and effort into?

2. Allen, despite early failures, never gave up on his goals. How do you react to early failures when you are attempting to reach your goal?

3. When you are not progressing toward your goal as fast as you want, what can you do to stay motivated?

Only those who dare to fail greatly can achieve greatly. -Robert F. Kennedy

Leading Through Challenges

Franklin Delano Roosevelt (FDR) was born in 1882 as an only child into a wealthy family that made their fortune in real estate and trade. FDR graduated from Harvard and became a lawyer. However, he found law practice boring and unchallenging and set his sights on greater challenges. He focused on politics and eventually accepted the nomination for vice president (as James M. Cox's running mate) at the 1920 Democratic Convention, but was defeated.

Just as his political career was beginning to soar, FDR was diagnosed with polio in 1921. Discouraged, he felt resigned to being a victim of polio, believing his political career to be over. With encouragement from his wife, he began a comeback. He was totally and permanently paralyzed from the waist down. Fitting his hips and legs with iron braces, he laboriously taught himself to walk a short distance by swiveling his torso while supporting himself with a cane. He was careful not to be seen in public using his wheelchair. Despite his efforts, he never regained the use of his legs.

He was elected governor of New York in 1928. By 1930, Republicans were being blamed for the Great Depression and FDR sensed opportunity. He began his run for the presidency, calling for government intervention in the economy to provide relief, recovery, and reform. His upbeat, positive approach and personal charm helped him win the presidency.

FDR kept his physical condition hidden to the public as much as possible. He felt that the leader of the most powerful country on earth should not show weakness by not being able to walk. In fact, it was a struggle for FDR to even stand. He usually appeared in public standing upright, while being supported on one side by an aide or one of his sons. When he spoke, a solid lectern was placed on the stage so that he could support himself on it; and as a result, he used his head to make gestures, because his hands were gripping the lectern.

Franklin Delano Roosevelt was the only president to be elected four times. Stricken with polio and barely able to stand, FDR overcame his disabilities to lead a nation through the Great Depression and World War II, greatly expanding the powers of the federal government through a series of programs and reforms known as the New Deal.

Affirmation: I will overcome.

To think about:

1. Today, disabilities are not hidden and are accepted by the public. Think of the difficulties people with disabilities face.

2. Do you ever take being healthy for granted?

3. FDR did not let his disabilities stop him in being a great leader of a powerful country. Do you let little things stop you? What can you learn from FDR?

The only thing we have to fear is fear itself. -Franklin D. Roosevelt

Learning is Relative

In elementary school, Albert Einstein excelled in his studies, enjoyed classical music, and playing the violin. However, he felt alienated and struggled with the rigid education he received. He also experienced a speech difficulty, a slow cadence in his speaking where he'd pause to consider what to say next.

In 1894, his family moved to Milan, Italy. However, Albert was left at a boarding house in Munich to finish his education. Alone, miserable, and facing military duty when he turned of age, Albert withdrew from school using a doctor's note to excuse him and went home to his parents. His parents were extremely concerned about the enormous problems that he would face as a school dropout and draft dodger with no employable skills.

Lacking the equivalent of a high school diploma, he failed much of the entrance exam to a Polytechnic School but got exceptional marks in mathematics and physics. Because of this, he was admitted to the school provided he completed his formal schooling first. He went to a special high school and eventually graduated, then faced a series of life challenges over the next few years. Because he liked to study on his own, he cut classes and earned the animosity of some of his professors, who wrote poor letters of recommendations that led to him being turned down for every academic position that he applied to after graduation. Albert was unemployed and desperate. He couldn't marry and support a family without a job, and his father's business had gone bankrupt. He took lowly jobs, but was unable to keep them.

Albert caught a break when he received a job at a patent office, evaluating patent applications for electromagnetic devices. The job allowed him to cultivate his interest in the transmission of electrical signals and electrical-mechanical synchronization. Albert would go on to develop the general theory of relativity. He is best known for his mass–energy equivalence formula, $E = mc^2$ (which has been dubbed "the world's most famous equation"), and he received the 1921 Nobel Prize in Physics for his services to theoretical physics.

Albert Einstein, who struggled to get a high school degree, turned in a career that generally makes him considered as the most influential physicist of the 20th century.

Affirmation: I like to try new things.

To think about:

1. How willing you are to try new things?

2. Albert Einstein was not afraid to make a mistake. How can you learn from a mistake?

3. Although Albert struggled in school, he had a passion for certain subjects. What subjects do you have a passion for?

A person who never made a mistake never tried anything new. -Albert Einstein

Life Tastes Good

As the Civil War he was fighting in drew to a close, a pharmacist named John "Doc" Pemberton wanted to invent something that would bring him commercial success. He invented many drugs, but none of them ever made any money. So, after a move to Atlanta, Doc decided to try his hand in the beverage market. Soda fountain drinks were becoming very popular, as the temperance movement had kept patrons out of bars.

Doc invented a type of coca wine, which contained a mixture of cocaine and wine. The original name of the drink was Pemberton's French Wine Coca. Doc sold the drink in various drugstores in Atlanta, claiming it as a product that provided clear thinking. With the advent of Prohibition, the alcohol content of the Wine Coca was removed and sold as a remedy to cure various ailments, such as headaches and upset stomachs. The drink did not do well in its first year, as Doc Pemberton had no idea how to advertise.

With his health failing, he sold some of the rights of his company to Asa Griggs Candler. Doc Pemberton died in August 1888, never seeing the commercial success he had dreamed of.

Candler tried a very innovative marketing technique. He hired traveling salesmen to pass out coupons for a free drink. His goal was for people to try the drink, like it, and buy it later on. He plastered logos on calendars, posters, notebooks, and bookmarks to reach customers on a large stage with a goal of going beyond a regional brand to make the drink a national brand. Candler wanted to sell the drink syrup as a patent medicine, claiming it would get rid of fatigue and headaches. But when Congress passed a tax on all medicines, the drink was no longer sold as a drug, but as a beverage.

What was this beverage that has such an interesting history and development? You've seen it advertised and you have most likely consumed it. The beverage that started out as a drug and touted as a cure-all for many ailments evolved into the largest soft drink producer in the world. People all over the world enjoy Coca-Cola today.

Affirmation: I adapt to changing situations.

To think about:

1. Coca-Cola has been very creative in their marketing. On a scale of 1-10 (1 low, 10 high), rate your creativity.

2. What creative things could you do in the next few weeks?

3. Coca-Cola marketed a "try it, you'll like it" philosophy, confident of their quality. How important is quality to you?

Life tastes good. -2001 Coca Cola ad

Long Walk to Freedom

Rolihlahla Nelson Mandela spent most of his life in prison. After all, the name Rolihlahla means "troublemaker." Born into a wealthy family in South Africa, his father lost his fortune when Nelson was an infant. His family was forced to move to a small village with no roads and live in a hut, surviving on eating beans and pumpkins.

For 20 years, Nelson directed a campaign of peaceful, non-violent defiance against the South African government and its racist policies of apartheid (enforced racial separation). He led a national workers strike in 1961. The South African government declared Nelson's organization a terrorist organization and he was arrested and sentenced to five years in prison for the strike. He was brought to trial again in 1963 and was sentenced to life imprisonment for political offenses, including sabotage.

Nelson was imprisoned for 27 years. As a black political prisoner, he was continuously abused and treated poorly. However, he was able to earn a Bachelor of Law degree through a University of London correspondence program while incarcerated and began to gain worldwide support for his unwavering beliefs.

After 22 years, he was offered his release in exchange for renouncing armed struggle, but he refused the offer. With increasing international pressure for his release, Nelson was eventually freed from prison after 27 years.

Four years later in 1994, South Africa held its first democratic elections. At age 77, Nelson Mandela was inaugurated as the country's first black president. Nelson Mandela won the Nobel Peace Prize for his work towards dismantling apartheid and published his autobiography, *Long Walk to Freedom*, much of which he had secretly written while in prison.

Nelson Mandela dedicated his entire life to a cause he strongly believed in. He was willing to give up 27 years of his life to accomplish his goal that all people should be treated equal.

Affirmation: I am committed to my goal.

To think about:

1. Nelson made a sacrifice of imprisonment to reach his goal. What sacrifices are you willing to make on your goals?

2. Nelson did not feel sorry for himself while in prison, but continued to better himself, preparing himself for future success. During challenging periods, do you keep in mind your overall goal and how each day brings you closer to it?

3. Nelson gained respect throughout the world. How do you gain respect?

It always seems impossible until it's done. -Nelson Mandela

Making a Difference

 Alfred was a Swedish chemist, engineer, and inventor. In 1895, he purchased an iron and steel mill, which he converted into a factory to manufacture military weapons. He invented ballistite, a smokeless military explosive, and cordite, a smokeless powder to replace gunpowder. Alfred developed an amazing 355 inventions involving weapons of destruction to be used by the military. His most famous invention used the explosive potential of nitroglycerin to form the explosive dynamite. He amassed a fortune selling supplies that eventually killed thousands in war.

Alfred was surprised one day to read his own obituary titled *"The Merchant of Death is Dead,"* in a French newspaper. He was surprised because he was still alive! It was Alfred's brother, Ludvig, who had died. The obituary was eight years premature for Alfred, but it made Alfred seriously think about his life. He was disappointed with what he read and concerned with how he would be remembered. Inspired to make a positive difference, he changed his will.

Alfred had spent most of his life inventing ammunitions and dynamite to be used in war, but surprisingly in his last will, he requested that his fortune be used to create a series of prizes for those who confer the "greatest benefit on mankind" in physics, chemistry, peace, physiology or medicine, and literature. He left millions of dollars to establish peace prizes.

Because of Alfred's reputation in manufacturing ammunitions, there was much skepticism surrounding the will, but finally the executors of his will formed the Nobel Foundation to take care of Alfred's fortune and organize the prizes. The man who had spent an entire life making war materials, Alfred Nobel, is now forever remembered for the Nobel Peace Prize.

Affirmation: I make a difference.

To think about:

1. What difference are you making in people's lives? Are you making positive or negative differences?

2. Late in life, Albert Nobel wanted to make a positive difference in life. In what ways can you make a positive difference in people's lives?

3. Albert eventually realized he was going down the wrong path. Are you headed down the right path? If not, what can you do to change the path you are going down?

Act as if what you do makes a difference. It does. -William James

Mistakes May Turn Out Well

George Crum, who was part African-American and part Native American, was working as a cook at the Moon Lake Lodge in Saratoga Springs in New York in the summer of 1853. French fries were on the lodge's menu because Thomas Jefferson had brought back the concept of the french fry from France in the late 1700s. The fried potatoes that were thickly sliced and were eaten with a fork were becoming very popular in America.

George was a tough, crusty old man who had worked as a trapper. If any of the diners at the Moon Lake Lodge complained about their food, George would send back any food that had been returned to his kitchen in an inedible state.

One day, a diner came into the lodge and ordered french fried potatoes. The man complained that the potatoes were too thick. Grumbling, George sliced the customer up a thinner batch of potatoes, fried them, and sent them back out to the dining room. The diner complained that they were still too thick and soft.

George, hoping to annoy the customer, took his sharp knife and sliced the potatoes as thin as he possibly could. He then fried the sliced potatoes in grease until they were hard and crunchy. There was no way now that the customer would be able to eat them with a fork! He sprinkled an over generous amount of salt on them, and sent them back to the unhappy customer.

The rest is history. The customer loved the thin, hard slices of fried potatoes, and the potato chip was born!

George Crum happily continued to make the thin, fried potatoes, calling them "Saratoga Chips" or "Potato Crunches." George opened his own restaurant that had a basket of potato chips on every table. They soon became so popular they were mass-produced, packaged in bags and sold as a snack.

Affirmation: I make the best out of mistakes.

To think about:

1. Have you ever had a mistake turn out well?

2. Are you willing to take risks to be successful?

3. How could not being afraid to fail lead to success?

If you're not making mistakes, then you're not doing anything. I'm positive that a doer makes mistakes. -John Wooden

Mount Everest—I'm Still Growing

In 1852, Mount Everest in the Himalayas was identified as the world's highest mountain at 29,000 feet. The idea of reaching "the roof of the world" was viewed as the ultimate feat.

The dangers of climbing Mount Everest include avalanches, crevasses, ferocious winds up to 125 miles per hour, sudden storms, temperatures of 40 degrees below zero, and oxygen deprivation. In the "death zone"—above 25,000 feet—the air holds only a third as much oxygen as at sea level, increasing the chances of hypothermia and frostbite. The lungs can fill up with fluid and the oxygen-starved brain can swell up. Even when breathing bottled oxygen, climbers experience extreme fatigue, impaired judgment and coordination, headaches, nausea, double vision, and sometimes hallucinations.

More than 200 people have lost their lives attempting to climb Mount Everest. The dead are left where they perish, because the effects of altitude make it nearly impossible to drag bodies off the mountain. Those ascending Everest pass through an icy graveyard littered with remnants of old tents and equipment, empty oxygen canisters, and frozen corpses.

Thirteen expeditions over a period of 30 years failed trying to reach the top of Mount Everest. Fifteen people lost their lives trying. In 1952, a New Zealand beekeeper, Edmund Hillary attempted to climb Mount Everest, but failed. A group in England asked him to address its members. Hillary walked on stage to a thunderous applause. The audience was recognizing an attempt at greatness, but Edmund Hillary saw himself as a failure. He moved away from the microphone and walked to the edge of the platform. He made a fist and pointed at a picture of the mountain, saying in a loud voice, "Mount Everest, you beat me the first time, but I'll beat you the next time because you've grown all you are going to grow...but I'm still growing!"

A year later, Hillary and Tenzing Norgay, an acclaimed Sherpa climber, became the first to reach the top of the world, when they climbed to the summit of Mount Everest.

Affirmation: I grow stronger every day.

To think about:

1. How do you grow daily?

2. After failing at a first attempt at something, how do you focus and motivate yourself to try again?

3. What is your Mount Everest? What is your commitment to achieve it?

Because it's there.
-George Mallory's (died attempting to climb Mount Everest) answer to the question 'Why do you want to climb Mt. Everest?'

Musical Genius

Ray Charles grew up in Georgia with his father a mechanic and his mother a sharecropper. Early in his childhood, Ray witnessed his brother drown. Things only got worse, and by the age of 7, Ray was blind. He attended the Florida School for the Deaf and the Blind where he learned to read, write, and arrange music in Braille. He also learned to play the piano, organ, sax, clarinet, and trumpet.

When he was 15, his mother died while he was on a music tour. Although gaining great music experience, he also picked up a heroin habit. At the age of 19, Ray's music career was taking off as he released his first music album and followed that up with several more. He was fast becoming a very popular musician.

The year 1960 brought Ray his first Grammy Award for "Georgia on My Mind," followed by another Grammy for the single, "Hit the Road, Jack."

Although he was achieving success in his musical career, his personal life was challenging, as he struggled with a heroin addiction. After being arrested for heroin possession, he finally kicked the habit at a clinic in Los Angeles.

Ray became a music legend recording more than 60 albums and performing more than 10,000 concerts. He was a music icon who was one of the first people inducted into the Rock and Roll Hall of Fame. He died of liver disease in 2004.

Ray Charles, called the "father of soul," overcame blindness and a heroin addiction to pioneer the genre of soul music and left a lasting impression on the music industry.

Affirmation: I learn from my failures.

To think about:

1. Ray was a very talented musician but worked extremely hard to use his ability. On a scale of 1-10, (1 low, 10 high) rate your ability level on three things you like to do.

2. How much of this ability was inherited?

3. How much of this ability came through practice, work and effort?

There are many spokes on the wheel of life. First, we're here to explore new possibilities.
-Ray Charles

Never Too Late

 Anna Moses was born to a family of 10 children and she gave birth to 10 children, five of whom died in infancy. Anna had a hard life working on a farm. Interested in art, she was creative, often using house paint to decorate and embroider pictures. When arthritis made it painful to use a needle, she turned to painting when she was in her late 70s.

She often painted scenes of rural life. She was able to capture the excitement of winter's first snow, Thanksgiving preparations and the new, young green of oncoming spring. Through her paintings, she taught thousands of people the value of a simple and uncomplicated manner of living that celebrated the virtues of American rural life.

At an age in life when most people are retired, she started to work professionally and thereby became an inspiration to senior citizens. She acquired the nickname, "Grandma Moses." She had been too busy all her life to bear the thought of being idle. She was a prolific painter, generating over 1,600 canvasses in three decades, 25 of them after she had passed her 100th birthday.

Before her fame, she would charge $2 for a small painting and $3 for a large one. Several years later, one of her paintings sold for $1.2 million! During the 1950s, Grandma Moses' exhibitions were so popular that they broke attendance records all over the world.

She demonstrated that age does not have to be a hindrance to a fulfilled life. In connection with Senior Citizens Month in May of 1969, honoring all older Americans, the U.S. government issued a stamp to commemorate Grandma Moses, a distinction given to few artists. On her 100th birthday in 1960, New York Governor Nelson Rockefeller proclaimed the day "Grandma Moses Day" in her honor.

Grandma Moses became a cultural icon. The spry, productive senior citizen was continually cited as an inspiration for housewives, widows, and retirees.

Affirmation: I make the most of my life.

To think about:

1. Grandma Moses didn't like to be idle. She was always working toward a goal. How productive are you in working toward your goals?

2. Why did Grandma Moses become a cultural icon to senior citizens?

3. What did you take out of the Grandma Moses story?

I look back on life like a good day's work, it was done and I feel satisfied with it. I was happy and contented; I knew nothing better and made the best out of what life offered. And life is what we make it, always has been, always will be. -Grandma Moses

No Limits

By the time George Dantzig reached high school, he was fascinated by geometry, an interest that was nurtured by his father, who liked to challenge him with complicated problems. George used his love for the challenge of mathematics to earn an undergraduate degree in mathematics and physics from the University of Maryland in 1936, and his master's degree in mathematics from the University of Michigan in 1938. He then enrolled in the doctoral program in mathematics at the University of California, Berkeley.

One day, George was running late to class. When he arrived, he noticed that his professor, Jerzy Neyman, had written two problems on the board. Dantzig assumed they were a homework assignment and wrote them down.

When he later went to do them, he found them a little harder than usual, but a few days later, he handed in completed solutions for the two problems, still believing that they were an assignment that was overdue. Later, George received a visit from his excited professor, eager to tell him that the homework problems he had solved were two of the most famous unsolved problems in statistics. What George thought was homework, turned out to be examples of famously unsolved statistics problems that his professor had used as examples on the blackboard.

George Dantzig went on to a have brilliant career and through his research in mathematical theory, computation, economic analysis, and applications to industrial problems, he made significant contributions to the development of linear programming.

Affirmation: I push past my limits.

To think about:

1. George Dantzig tackled previously unsolved problems thinking it was just homework. He had no limiting thoughts. What limits do you place on yourself?

2. How could you remove the limits you place on yourself?

3. How can you break down big problems into smaller parts to find a workable solution?

Limits only exist in the mind.

Overcoming Dyslexia

Tom Mathoper spent his childhood being bullied and trying to hide his dyslexia from his peers. His family was poor and had to move around a lot while his father looked for work. Young Tom spent his boyhood eternally on the move, and by the time he was 14, he had attended 15 different schools in the United States and Canada. When he reached high school, he could barely read. He dreamed of becoming an actor and appeared in a number of plays while in high school, but struggle to read the roles. He focused on athletics and competed in many sports, playing hockey, baseball, wrestling, soccer, and football. However, a knee injury stopped his hopes of pursuing an athletic career.

At the age of 19, he received an acting job. As he embraced his love of acting, he realized that his inability to read would have a negative effect if he didn't work to overcome it.

He eventually adopted L. Ron Hubbard's learning method of "Study Technology," which helped him develop his reading and study habits.

He trained to focus his attention and learned how to create mental images in order to comprehend what he read. Tom refused to let his dyslexia stand in the way of his acting career. With great drive and determination, he continued to pursue his dream of becoming an actor.

Thomas Mapother came a long way from the lonely wanderings of his youth. Tom Mapother was Tom Cruise Mapother, better known as simply Tom Cruise, who overcame a challenge to become one of the most famous actors and producers ever.

Affirmation: I turn my weaknesses into strengths.

To think about:

1. How important is your education?

2. Have you ever struggled academically? How did your effort and attitude help you achieve?

3. Pride is a tremendous resource. How proud are you? How does that pride affect your performance?

I love what I do. I take great pride in what I do. And I can't do something half-way, three-quarters, nine-tenths. If I'm going to do something, I go all the way. -Tom Cruise

Persistence of Lincoln

One of the greatest examples in history of persistence is Abraham Lincoln.

Born into poverty, Lincoln was faced with defeat throughout his life. He lost numerous elections, failed in business, and suffered a nervous breakdown. He could have quit numerous times, but he didn't. Because he didn't quit, he became one of the greatest presidents in the history of our country. His road to becoming a significant part of history included:

- 1816- Family forced out of home and he had to work to support them.
- 1818- His mother died
- 1832- Lost his job
- 1832- Defeated for legislature
- 1833- Borrowed money to begin business, and went bankrupt
- 1834- Elected to legislature
- 1835- Engaged to be married and his sweetheart died
- 1836- Had nervous breakdown
- 1838- Defeated for speaker of the state legislature
- 1844- Ran for congress, lost
- 1846- Ran for congress again, won
- 1849- Rejected for Land Officer
- 1854- Defeated for Senate
- 1856- Defeated for nomination for Vice-President
- 1858- Again defeated for Senate
- 1860- Elected President

Affirmation: I will succeed.

To think about:

1. Think of a failure you have had in life. How has that motivated you to achieve success?

2. After repeated failures, what do you often say to yourself?

3. Think of three things you can do to recover from failure.

Nothing in this world can take the place of persistence. Talent will not; nothing is more common than unsuccessful people with talent. Genius will not; unrewarded genius is almost a proverb. Education will not; the world is full of educated derelicts. Persistence and determination alone are omnipotent. The slogan "press on" has solved and always will solve the problems of the human race. -Calvin Coolidge

Playing with One Hand

Jim Abbott had a very successful career as a baseball pitcher. He established himself as a national hero in college by being named the top amateur baseball player in the nation. He pitched and won the gold medal baseball exhibition game in the 1988 Olympics Games. He skipped the minors and accomplished the rare feat of immediately becoming a starter in his first year of professional baseball. He pitched a no-hitter for the New York Yankees, a feat few Hall of Famers ever achieve. His 87 career wins and a 4.25 earned run average could be considered just average for a professional baseball player. However, Jim Abbott was not your average ballplayer. He had as much of an impact as any player who played the game, giving renewed hope to thousands of people.

Jim Abbott was born with a deformed arm. He played baseball without a right hand. His right arm ended where his wrist should have been. He pitched with a right-handed fielder's glove perched pocket-down over the end of his stubbed right arm. After his delivery, he would slip his left hand into the glove and be ready to field the ball. After catching the ball, he would hold the glove against his chest in the crook of his right arm and extract the ball with his left hand, ready to make another throw. Observers were amazed at how smoothly and efficiently he could catch and throw the ball with one hand.

But Jim had developed the ability to overcome his handicaps by hard work that allowed him to do with one hand what others did with two. He spent hours throwing a rubber ball against the brick wall and catching it on the rebound. His father helped him develop the technique for handling his glove-hand switch, which allowed Jim to throw and catch the ball with the same hand. When Jim began school, he was fitted with a mechanical hand made of fiberglass and metal. The hook frightened some of his classmates and made him self-conscious, and he hated wearing it. Eventually, his parents stopped making him wear it.

People have described Abbott's life as courageous, motivational and inspirational. The all-around athlete did more with one hand than many players dream of doing with two. But for Jim Abbott, he did it for the love of the game.

Affirmation: I love what I do.

To think about:

1. Despite physical handicaps, Jim persevered. Do you take your physical abilities for granted?

2. Jim did not accept excuses. Have you been limited in the past by excuses?

3. Jim's story gave hope to thousands. How does it give hope and inspiration to you?

Find something you love in this world, and don't let anyone ever change your opinion that you can do it. -Jim Abbott

Real Horror Story

An unconscious man lay in a Victorian mansion haunted by bats shrieking in the rafters. Drunk and high from snorting so much cocaine, his nose had become a gushing fountain of blood soaking the front of his shirt. The scene was just like a Stephen King novel. Ironic, since it was Stephen King. He had written over 63 books in 35 years, including best-sellers, such as *Carrie*, *The Shining*, and *The Green Mile*, which had been turned into blockbuster movies. One of the world's most successful authors, he had an estimated fortune of $135 million.

Why would a successful millionaire end up an alcohol and a drug addict? For Stephen King, the alcohol and drugs provided him an escape from unhappiness he had endured growing up in poverty as a child. His father left the family when he was 2 years old, and King was fearful his mother would do the same. He had nightmares at home and developed paranoia about death. His only way to deal with the bogeyman was to write about him. Unfortunately, writing wasn't the only way of escaping reality he used. He tried marijuana, speed, and LSD.

Stephen became frustrated after receiving a string of rejection letters from publishers and took out his anger on his children. The death of his mother sent him into a deep depression. Believing that if he wrote about something bad, it would never happen, he wrote *The Shining*, the story of a little boy whose alcoholic father tries to kill him.

He worried that he might be unable to write without being drunk and developed new phobias of snakes, rats, and small spaces. He drank heavily and used so much cocaine that he had to stick cotton wool up his nose to stop the bleeding on to his typewriter. He got to the point he was only sober a few hours a day and often contemplating suicide. He realized if he didn't change his ways, it would probably cost him his family, and even his life. After many attempts and broken promises to go clean, he finally did, and his greatest fear came true: he could no longer write.

Throughout many difficult nights and days, he began to write one word at a time until, little by little, his ability to tell a story returned. Stephen King, one of the greatest writers of all-time, was successful in a career marked by personal challenges.

Affirmation: I keep working to be the person I want to be.

To think about:

1. Nobody is perfect, but it is possible to strive to be the person you dream to be. What strides are you taking towards your dream?

2. How do get back after a set-back to meet the next challenge?

3. Do you believe that money equals success? Why or why not?

Talent is cheaper than table salt. What separates the talented individual from the successful one is a lot of hard work. -Stephen King

Revolutionary Vision

When Henry Ford was 15 years old, his father gave him a pocket watch, which the young boy took apart and reassembled. His watch re-assembly was only a glimpse of what was to come. Unsatisfied with farm work, Henry left home at the age of 16 to take an apprenticeship as a machinist in Detroit.

Eventually, Henry developed his plans for a horseless carriage, and in 1896, he constructed his first model, the Ford Quadricycle. After a few trials building cars and companies, in 1903, Henry Ford established the Ford Motor Company. Henry became renowned for his revolutionary vision; the manufacture of an inexpensive automobile made by skilled workers who earn steady wages.

In 1914, he sponsored the development of the moving assembly line technique of mass production, which revolutionized the industry. Simultaneously, he introduced the $5-per-day wage as a method of keeping the best workers loyal to his company. Simple to drive and cheap to repair, half of all cars in America in 1918 were Ford Model Ts.

Henry Ford died of a cerebral hemorrhage in 1947, but his visionary methods are credited today for helping to build America's economy during the nation's vulnerable early years.

Affirmation: My vision guides me to success.

To think about:

1. Henry had a vision that made history. Where will your vision take you?

2. What does the phrase "fail to plan, plan to fail" mean to you?

3. How might you work out your plan?

Coming together is a beginning; keeping together is progress; working together is success.
-Henry Ford

Rough Rider

When Theodore Roosevelt was a young boy, doctors discovered that he had a weak heart, and advised him to avoid vigorous activity. Teddy spent a lot of time inside his family's house due to his many illnesses and asthma, and in addition, he was home-schooled. Teddy and his father developed a close bond and his father developed a rigorous physical routine for him that included weightlifting and boxing. This set the stage for Teddy to eventually live and enjoy an active physical life.

When his father died during his second year at Harvard, he channeled his grief into working even harder: He enrolled at Columbia Law School and got married. He didn't stay long at law school, leaving to join the New York State Assembly as a representative from New York City, becoming the youngest to serve in that position. However, the tragic deaths of his mother and his wife, which occurred on the same day (February 14, 1884), prompted him to leave for the Dakota Territory for two years. There, he lived as a cowboy and cattle rancher, leaving his infant daughter in the care of his elder sister.

Teddy returned to New York and went back to work in government, but left his post to organize a volunteer cavalry known as the Rough Riders during the Spanish-American War. He led a bold charge up San Juan Hill in the Battle of San Juan Heights and became a war hero. He was eventually elected governor of New York. He became the vice president of the United States and when William McKinley was assassinated in 1901, Teddy Roosevelt became the youngest man to assume the U.S. presidency at age 42. Roosevelt's presidency focused on prosecuting monopolies under the Sherman Antitrust Act, civil rights, supporting desegregation, women's suffrage and the environment.

From a slow start in his childhood, Teddy Roosevelt's energetic vision helped create millions of acres of national forest and parkland, which millions of people have enjoyed.

Affirmation: I dare mighty things.

To think about:

1. Teddy overcame childhood illness to be a very physically active person. Do you think there is a relationship between mind and body?

2. Teddy was a leader by example. What kind of example do you set for others to follow?

3. President Roosevelt had a vision of creating national parks. His vision has led to the enjoyment of many. What things do you do that others can enjoy?

Far better is it to dare mighty things, to win glorious triumphs, even though checkered by failure... than to rank with those poor spirits who neither enjoy nor suffer much, because they live in a gray twilight that knows not victory nor defeat. -Theodore Roosevelt

Rough Road to Success

Oprah Winfrey grew up in a troubled adolescence in a small farming community in Mississippi. She was sexually abused by a number of male relatives and friends of her mother. She moved to Nashville to live with her father, entered Tennessee State University in 1971, and began working in radio and television broadcasting in Nashville.

At the age of 22, she was fired from her job as a television reporter because she was "unfit for TV." She landed a TV chat show *People Are Talking*. The show became a hit and Winfrey was able to host her own morning show, *A.M. Chicago*. Her success led to nationwide fame and a role in the film, *The Color Purple*, for which she was nominated for an Academy Award for Best Supporting Actress.

Oprah launched the *Oprah Winfrey Show* in 1986 as a nationally syndicated program and drew large audiences, and with it, much financial success. Oprah continued to garner success and popularity with her own television network and book club. She also became known for her weight loss efforts and competed in the Marine Corps Marathon.

Oprah is a dedicated activist for children's rights and received the nation's highest civilian honor, the Presidential Medal of Freedom in 2013.

Oprah Winfrey endured a rough and abusive childhood as well as numerous career setbacks on her road to a position of popularity, fortune, and fame.

Affirmation: I chart my own course.

To think about:

1. Oprah did not let early failures stop her. If others tell you you are not good enough, what stages do you go through to bounce back?

2. Oprah has given away her money and time for charity. If you don't have money to give, how can you give back with your time?

3. Oprah has worked hard to be physically fit and in shape. How important is being physically fit to you?

The greatest discovery of all time is that a person can change his future by merely changing his attitude. -Oprah Winfrey

Soul Surfer

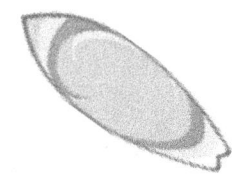

Bethany Hamilton was born to be a surfer. Born into a family of surfers in Hawaii, she began surfing at a young age. At the age of 8, Bethany entered her first surf competition and won, sparking a love for surfing competition. At the age of 13, Bethany was attacked by a 14-foot tiger shark while surfing off Kauai's North Shore. Bethany lost her left arm and over 60 percent of her blood. After several successful surgeries, coupled with a positive attitude, Bethany was on her way to recovery.

Miraculously, just one month after the attack, Bethany returned to the water to continue pursuing her goal to become a professional surfer. She made her return to surf competition just over a year after the attack, taking first place in the Explorer Women's division of the 2005 National Surfing Championships—her first national title.

In 2007, Bethany realized her dream and turned pro. Since losing her arm, Bethany's story has been told in hundreds of stories and she has been recognized with numerous awards, public appearances, and various speaking engagements. Bethany shared her life story in her autobiography titled *Soul Surfer*. Seven years later, the book was made into a movie.

Bethany Hamilton has grown from a young teenage girl who survived a shark attack into a professional surfer with a shining beacon of inspiration and hope. Bethany has touched millions of people with her inspirational message, charitable efforts, and overall spirit.

Affirmation: My soul always shines.

To think about:

1. What type of inspiration and hope did Bethany's story give to you?

2. Only one month after a shark attack took her arm, Bethany returned to surfing. How can passion and effort overcome obstacles?

3. Bethany has the heart of a champion. What does it mean to have the heart of a champion?

Courage, sacrifice, determination, commitment, toughness, heart, talent, guts. That's what little girls are made of; the heck with sugar and spice. -Bethany Hamilton, Soul Surfer: A True Story of Faith, Family, and Fighting to Get Back on the Board

Starry Starry Night

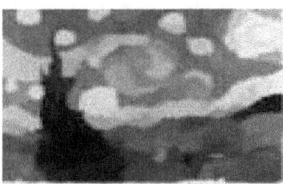 At the age of 15, Vincent van Gogh was forced to leave school and go to work because his family was struggling financially. He got a job at his uncles' art dealership. He had learned to speak French, German, and English, as well as his native Dutch. He eventually transferred to an art gallery in London and fell in love, only to have his marriage proposal rejected, which led to a nervous breakdown. He became angry with people at work, telling customers not to buy the "worthless art," and was eventually fired. He threw away all his books except for his Bible, and devoted his life to God.

For a while, he volunteered to move to an impoverished coal mine in the south of Belgium, a place where preachers were usually sent as punishment. He preached and ministered to the sick, and also drew pictures of the miners and their families. Eventually, he moved to Belgium and became an artist. Though he had no formal art training, he began studying on his own. He lived a nomadic life, moving throughout the region while drawing and painting the landscape and its people before moving to France. He spent his money on paint rather than food. He lived on coffee and bread, and was known to have sipped on turpentine and eat paint.

Vincent struggled with mental illness, once cutting off part of his own ear. He remained poor and virtually unknown throughout his life, having only sold one painting his entire life. He died at age 37, from a self-inflicted gunshot wound.

After his death, his paintings were displayed at a show in Paris, and his fame subsequently grew enormously as he was hailed as an artist and a genius.

He completed more than 2,100 works, consisting of 860 oil paintings and more than 1,300 watercolors, drawings and sketches. Several of his paintings rank among the most expensive in the world; "Irises" sold for a record $53.9 million, and his "Portrait of Dr. Gachet" sold for $82.5 million, after his death.

Affirmation: I enjoy my life.

To think about:

1. Vincent was a self-made artist and taught himself on his own. To be successful, what extra things will you do?

2. Vincent van Gogh was so passionate he didn't eat right. Is it possible to be too passionate?

3. How do you keep your goals and a happy, successful life in perspective?

What would life be if we had no courage to attempt anything? -Vincent Van Gogh

Successful Act

Sydney Poitier barely survived the first few months of his life. Born prematurely, he grew up on a tiny island in the Bahamas without electricity, running water, automobiles, or other modern day conveniences. His education was sporadic, as he occasionally attended a one-room schoolhouse but learned very little, leaving school at age 12 to help his family. Without an education, his career options appeared extremely limited.

Sydney faced racial discrimination in the south, so he moved to New York. He was 16 years old with only a few dollars. He slept in bus stations until he earned enough money for a room. Finally, to escape the cold, Sydney joined the Army, but he didn't fit in and he faked insanity to receive a medical discharge. He appeared to be trapped with no money, no job, and no education.

He auditioned for a role in a theater but was ridiculed because of his Caribbean accent and poor reading skills. The rejection would be a turning point in his life. He viewed the rejection as a challenge and was determined to prove that he could act. He set a goal to improve his reading and worked long hours reading newspapers between his shifts as a dishwasher. He listened to the radio for hours and repeated every word to modify his accent. Sydney returned back to the theater where he was rejected and exchanged janitor work for acting classes. Finally, Sydney got a break when the star of the show wasn't able to act one night, and Sydney filled in. His hard work had prepared him, and he seized the opportunity to be successful.

Sydney went on to be a successful actor and then appear in films. Historically, American films had limited black actors to the roles of servants in a demeaning light, but Sydney started to change that. He struggled for several years, supplementing his acting work with poorly paid day jobs. He desperately needed money, but he turned down roles that portrayed blacks in a poor light and robbed them of their character.

Opportunities slowly began to improve for black actors in the 1950s, and Sydney Poitier became the top African American star of the era and was the first black actor to win an Academy Award. Later in his career, President Obama selected him to receive the nation's highest civilian honor, the Presidential Medal of Freedom.

Affirmation: I continue to learn and get better.

To think about:

1. Sydney was rejected for roles early in his career, but only worked harder to succeed. Do you believe hard work leads to success?

2. List three steps that you could achieve to improve in a chosen area.

3. Sydney Poitier was considered a class act. What does that mean?

If I'm remembered for having done a few good things and if my presence here has sparked some good energies, that's plenty. -Sydney Poitier

Trailblazing

 Sam grew up on a farm in Oklahoma during the depression and knew that hard work and thrift were a way of life. His parents decided that the farm was not profitable enough to raise a family on and moved to Missouri. Sam developed into a leader as he grew up. He played basketball and led his football team to the state title as the starting quarterback. He also served as the student body president his senior year in high school. He had to help support his family, along with his father and brother, because money was lacking due to the depression. Sam's job was to milk the family cow, bottle the milk, deliver the surplus to customers, and then deliver newspapers afterwards.

After high school, Sam attended the University of Missouri. Money for school was hard to come by, so Sam waited tables in exchange for meals, lifeguarded at the school pool, and also delivered newspapers. After college graduation, he worked at J.C. Penney as a management trainee, earning a salary of $75 a month. After military duty, he opened his own department store with a $20,000 loan from his father-in-law. Sam focused on providing a wide range of goods at discounted prices to the consumer and keeping his stores open longer than his competitors, even during the Christmas season. His lower-priced strategies and the idea of self-service allowed him to drive up sales and negotiate lower prices on purchases with his wholesalers.

Discount marketing requires a large customer base, but the problem in Bentonville, Arkansas was that there were only 3,000 people. Sam's answer to that challenge was to open 16 stores in other small towns. Sam's next challenge was to get around to all his stores, so he learned to fly a plane. One store led to another and then another, and in the next 30 years, more than 1,500 stores were built. Sam's enthusiasm, hard work, and willingness to think and act "outside the box" led him to the top of the business world to become one of the richest men in the world as the founder of **WAL-MART**!

Sam Walton liked taking calculated risks, but by his own admission, 90 percent of the time, his trailblazing in new directions did not work, but the 10 percent of the time that it did, it was worth it. Sam believed mistakes and failures along the way were inevitable and both good and bad experiences can teach us, and if we learn from those experiences that will make us better.

Affirmation: I try new ideas.

To think about:

1. Sam Walton was a trailblazer who tried new ideas. What new ideas do you have?

2. Do you have a plan to follow up on your ideas?

3. Think of an obstacle that you were able to overcome. Was there a different way you could have overcome the problem that involved thinking "outside the box?"

I had to pick myself up and get on with it, do it all over again, only even better this time.
-Sam Walton

Triumph of an American Dreamer

As a child, Walt Disney began drawing, painting, and selling pictures of neighbors and family friends. He learned to work hard, beginning when he had to wake up at 3:00 a.m. to deliver the daily newspaper. He loved to dream and imagine; traits that he would carry with him his entire life. When Walt was 16, his father started a small factory and wanted Walt to work in it, but Walt wanted to be a cartoonist. However, Walt wanted to serve his country first and dropped out of school at age 16 to join the Army, but was rejected for being underage. So he joined the Red Cross as an ambulance driver.

After the war, Walt's average ability in drawings was not enough to get him a job. Determined to be a cartoonist, he taught himself film animation and eventually opened his own film animation company. But through poor management, the film company went bankrupt. Walt realized he was just average in drawing, but his strength was his tremendous imagination. With his brother Roy, he moved to Hollywood and began working at a studio, but again found himself without money. Refusing to give up, he created a cartoon character called Mickey Mouse and turned him into an instant celebrity. This one cartoon character soon turned Walt's business into one of the most powerful and influential companies on the planet.

Walt Disney was an extraordinary individual whose imagination transformed the world. Walt set out on a dream that almost nobody believed could be achieved. He wanted to create a land of imagination and fantasy that would bring joy to millions around the world. It would be his greatest challenge and life's work. His idea of Disneyland was met with critics and was known as Walt's folly before it opened. After Disneyland was opened, Walt continued to dream, planning Disneyworld. However, Disneyworld did not open until a year after his death.

Walt Disney delivered products and services that inspired the human imagination with what could be accomplished if one sets their heart and minds to achieving positive results. He was an innovator, filmmaker, storyteller, showman, and educator who made it his mission in life to create family fun in his own unique way. Through his hard work and optimism, Walt Disney not only fulfilled his dreams, but the dreams of Americans.

Affirmation: I follow my dreams.

To think about:

1. Walt Disney was a visionary. What is your vision?

2. Where do you see yourself five years from now? Ten years? Twenty-five years?

3. Having a dream and following up on the dream are two different things. How do you plan to pursue and achieve your dreams?

All the adversity I've had in my life, all the troubles and obstacles have strengthened me. You may not realize it when it happens, but sometimes a kick in the teeth may be the best thing for you. -Walt Disney

This Seat is Mine

 Rosa Parks experienced racial discrimination growing up with her mother and grandparents. Her grandparents were former slaves and strong advocates for racial equality. Rosa recalled her grandfather standing in front of their house with a shotgun while Ku Klux Klan members marched down the street. Rosa attended a segregated one-room school in Alabama. Her school lacked basic supplies such as desks. African-American students were forced to walk to the schoolhouse while the city provided bus transportation to a new school building for the white students. Rosa attended segregated schools in Montgomery, Alabama, but had to leave school in the 11th grade to attend to both her sick grandmother and mother and never returned to public school. She did eventually earn her high school diploma.

The Montgomery Alabama City Code required that all public transportation be segregated and the bus drivers had the powers of a police officer to carry out the code. The white passengers were seated in the front of the bus and the African-American passengers in the back. When the seats in the front of the bus filled up and more white passengers got on, the bus driver would ask black passengers to give up their seat.

On December 1, 1955, after a long day's work at a Montgomery department store where she worked as a seamstress, Rosa Parks was riding the bus home. Eventually, the bus was full and the driver noticed that several white passengers were standing in the aisle. He stopped the bus and asked four black passengers to give up their seats. Three complied, but Rosa refused and remained seated. The driver called the police and had her arrested. Later, Rosa recalled that her refusal wasn't because she was physically tired, but that she was tired of giving in.

Rosa's arrest set off protests. African-Americans refused to ride the busses. Some people carpooled and others rode in African-American operated cabs, but most of the estimated 40,000 African-American commuters living in the city at the time had opted to walk to work, some as far as 20 miles. The boycotts lead to protests and riots. In June of 1956, the district court declared racial segregation laws (also known as "Jim Crow laws") unconstitutional.

Rosa Park's quiet and courageous act changed American and re-directed the course of history.

Affirmation: I stand up for what I believe in.

To think about:

1. Rosa made a stand for what she believed in. What do you stand for?

2. What are you willing to do to stand for your beliefs?

3. Rosa changed America with quiet courage. What is quiet courage? How could you display quiet courage?

Each person must live their life as a model for others. -Rosa Parks

Turning Bad Luck Into Good Luck

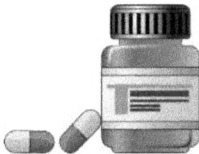

At the age of 16, while working in a local shoe factory, Charles Walgreen accidentally cut off the top joint of his middle finger, ending his athletic career. Were it not for the accident, Charles career as a pharmacist may never have happened. The doctor who treated Charles took a liking to him and persuaded him to become a druggist's apprentice. His first pharmacy experience was a failure, and Charles left after just a year and a half on the job.

He became a registered pharmacist by working in a drug store during the day and studying pharmacy at night. He joined the military to fight in the Spanish-American War, during which time he contracted malaria. The disease left him in poor health for many years, but he was able to buy interest in a pharmacy, which he renamed C.R. Walgreen Company.

Slowly, the company added stores, and when Charles died in 1939, there were 493 stores. Although many of the things we see today look obvious, Charles Walgreen introduced them to the world. His stores were well lit and clean. He paid great attention to small details. He made great improvements in the open display of merchandise and introduced display counters that enabled customers to pick out merchandise for themselves.

Charles Walgreen, the man whose bad luck turned into good fortune, went from owning a small neighborhood drugstore to owning one of the most respected American corporations.

Affirmation: I make my own luck.

To think about:

1. Charles used his bad luck of a finger injury and turned it into good luck. How have you turned bad luck into something good?

2. Charles paid great attention to small detail. How do the little things add up to matter?

3. Charles had many innovative ideas that seem obvious today. What innovative ideas might you have?

We believe in working, not waiting; in laughing, not weeping; in boosting, not knocking and in the pleasure of selling products. -Charles Walgreen

Unlock Your Mind

 Harry Houdini was a master magician, as well as a fabulous locksmith. He is known as the most famous escape artist in the world. He would free himself from jails, handcuffs, chains, ropes, and straitjackets often while hanging from a rope in plain sight of street audiences. He moved on to greater challenges, escaping from locked, water-filled milk cans and his most famous act, the Chinese Water Torture Act, in which he was suspended upside-down in a locked glass-and-steel cabinet full to overflowing with water. The act required that Houdini hold his breath for more than three minutes. The possibility of failure and death thrilled his audiences.

Houdini was very confident in his talents. He claimed that he could escape from any jail cell in the world in less than an hour. In order to build interest in his traveling show, the great escape artist Houdini would frequently arrive in a town early and challenge the local jailer to try to keep him locked in a cell. If he couldn't escape within an hour, he would offer the jailer a $1,000 reward. Every time he was given this challenge, he did just as he promised, and in a few short minutes he would miraculously escape, except for one time.

A small town in the British Isles built a new jail cell and they were proud of it. "Come give us a try," they said to Houdini, and he agreed. He walked into the prison cell full of confidence. He had done this hundreds of times before. Inside his belt, Houdini held a special lock pick he had designed. Once the jail cell was closed, Houdini took off his coat, and set to work with his lock pick. But he discovered that something was unusual about this particular lock. For 30 minutes he worked and got nowhere. His confidence began to disappear.

An hour passed, and still he had not been able to open the door. He was frustrated and bathed in sweat, unable to pick the lock. He tried all the tricks of his trade but nothing worked. After two hours and totally exhausted, Houdini literally collapsed against the door. The door swung open and he discovered it had not been locked in the first place! It was locked only to him in his mind.

Affirmation: I live with an open mind.

To think about:

1. Do you convince yourself that you cannot do something before you even start?

2. What limits do you have in your mind that could limit how you perform?

3. What doors lay ahead of you? How will you prepare to go through them?

The will to win, the desire to succeed, the urge to reach your full potential, these are the keys that will unlock the door to personal excellence. -Confucius

Wear the Red

The Lakota Indians were known as great warriors. The warriors were expected to provide for and defend the family. The Lakota men took great pride in becoming warriors, for that is how they gained prestige and family honor. In order to become a warrior, a young Lakota boy had to pass a series of challenges. The physical challenges were difficult and not all those invited were able to pass. The first challenges allowed the young warriors to demonstrate the skills of battle such as horsemanship and marksmanship. But the last challenge truly tested the elite and was the most difficult test of endurance. The challenge had a time limit of four days and was done during the hottest part of the year. Each young warrior was sent out by himself, without food or water and only had a knife for protection and was told to follow a well-known path to a high cliff. Once the warrior reached the cliff, they were instructed to climb to the top of the cliff and recover a red sash that had been tied to a stone at the top of the mountain. The goal was to recover the sash from the top of the cliff and return it to the camp within the four-day time period.

The endurance challenge was very difficult, and because of the great distances they would have to travel, the young warriors would usually get back by sunset of the fourth day, exhausted, thirsty, and hungry. As soon as they arrived in camp, they were asked to present the sash they had recovered. The sash was held tightly in their hands. The young warrior held one end of the sash at head height and let it unfurl toward the ground. If it extended all the way to the ground, the young man was considered a Red Shirt Warrior. If it did not reach the ground, he was not a Red Shirt Warrior and would never again be allowed another opportunity to join the elite group. No explanation was given to the ones denied and no explanation was ever needed, because it wasn't just a test of endurance, but more importantly a test of honor.

To be a Red Shirt Warrior, not only did one need to meet the physical challenge, but more importantly, to meet the moral challenge of honor. At the cliff, one sash was tied to a stone at the top and when it was unfurled from the man's head, it easily reached the ground. Another sash was tied to a tree located half way up the cliff, at a place where the young man could stop and rest in the shade. That sash was the shorter of two and when it was unfurled in front of the elders of the Red Shirt Warriors, it told the story that the young man being tested had taken a short cut. He had not gone the full distance. He had not completed the challenge.

Affirmation: I am a person of honor.

To think about:

1. What does it mean to "wear the red?"

2. Would you pass the endurance test to be Red Shirt Warrior?

3. In a list of important facts about you, where would honor be on the list?

No person was ever honored for what he received. Honor has been the reward for what he gave. -Calvin Coolidge

Wonder of it All

 As a result of receiving too much oxygen in the incubator as a premature baby, Stevland Hardaway Judkins was blinded. Born in 1950, two months premature, Stevie was placed in an incubator for life support. However, an excess of oxygen resulted in the scarring and detachment of his retina, leading to a condition known as retinopathy of prematurity.

From his challenging start, his positive attitude and work ethic landed him a spot in the Rock and Roll Hall of Fame.

Stevie showed an early gift for music and before the age of 10, he had taught himself to play the harmonica, piano, and drums. He signed a record deal with Motown and his first album was released when he was only 12 years old. Despite the early success, Stevie wasn't content to sit on his laurels. He studied classical piano and continually worked to improve his musical abilities and songwriting capabilities.

Due in part to his own innate talent, but also his deep commitment to his craft, Stevie stayed relevant as a singer and musician as he went from boy to man. In 1971, Stevie, who'd begun writing his own music, negotiated a new contract with Motown that gave him almost total control over his records and greatly increased his royalty rate.

In the 1970s, Stevie won an incredible 15 Grammys. He has won 24 Grammys and was awarded the Grammy Lifetime Achievement Award in 1996. He has also earned the Academy and Golden Globe awards for his soundtracks to movies.

Stevie Wonder, the little boy who overcame blindness and showed an incredible talent early, coupled with a strong desire to learn, became one of the greatest personalities in music history.

Affirmations: My hard work makes me better.

To think about:

1. What happens when you combine talent and effort?

2. Would you rather be knows as someone with a lot of talent or someone who gives a great effort?

3. Stevie was blind from birth. Do you take things such as sight for granted? Be thankful for the things you have.

You can't base your life on other people's expectations. -Stevie Wonder

World's Toughest Race

Every year, Australia hosts a 544-mile endurance run from Sydney to Melbourne. It is considered among the world's most grueling ultra-marathons. The race takes five days to complete and is normally only attempted by world-class athletes who train specifically for the event. These athletes are typically less than 40 years old and sponsored by large companies such as Nike. In 1983, a man named Cliff Young showed up at the start of this race. Cliff was 61 years old and wore overalls and work boots. To everyone's shock, Cliff wasn't a spectator. He picked up his race number and joined the other runners.

The press and other athletes became curious and questioned Cliff. They told him, "You're crazy, there's no way you can finish this race." To which he replied, "Yes, I can. See, I grew up on a farm where we couldn't afford horses or tractors, and the whole time I was growing up, whenever the storms would roll in, I'd have to go out and round up the sheep. We had 2,000 sheep on 2,000 acres. Sometimes I would have to run those sheep for two or three days. It took a long time, but I'd always catch them. I believe I can run this race."

When the race started, the pros quickly left Cliff behind. The crowds and television audience were entertained because Cliff didn't even run properly; he appeared to shuffle. Many even feared for the old farmer's safety. All of the professional athletes knew that it took about 5 days to finish the race. In order to compete, one had to run about 18 hours a day and sleep the remaining 6 hours. The thing is, Cliff Young didn't know that!

When the morning of the second day came, everyone was in for another surprise. Not only was Cliff still in the race, he had continued jogging all night. Eventually, Cliff was asked about his tactics for the rest of the race. To everyone's disbelief, he claimed he would run straight through to the finish without sleeping. Each night, he moved a little closer to the leading pack. By the final night, he had surpassed all of the young, world-class athletes. He was the first competitor to cross the finish line, and he set a new course record. The Sydney to Melbourne race is still run today and modern competitors do not sleep. Winning the race requires runners to go all night as well as all day, just like Cliff Young.

Affirmation: I step up to the challenge and my body responds.

To think about:

1. What sacrifices are you willing to make to be successful?

2. When things get tough, what keeps you going?

3. Are you persistent enough to reach your goals? If so, why do you think so.

Crossing the starting line may be an act of courage, but crossing the finish line is an act of faith. Faith is what keeps us going when nothing else will. -John Bingham

While I Pondered Weak and Weary

Within three years of Edgar Allan Poe's birth, both of his parents had died, and he was taken in by the wealthy tobacco merchant, John Allan, and his wife in Richmond, Virginia while Edgar's siblings went to live with other families.

Edgar showed a great interest in writing and began composing poetry at age 13. He started college at the University of Virginia but didn't have enough money to pay expenses. To make enough money, he began gambling and lost, going into great debt and was forced to withdraw from college. Discouraged, he went home to Richmond to discover his fiancée had become engaged to another man.

A few years later, he started at West Point, but was thrown out after only eight months. Edgar was living in poverty but started publishing and eventually gained an editorial position at the Southern Literary Messenger in Richmond. It was at this magazine that he finally found his life's work as a magazine writer. He was the first well-known American writer to try to earn a living through writing alone, resulting in a financially difficult life and career.

He became a champion for the cause of higher wages for writers, as well as for an international copyright law. Best known for his tales of mystery, Poe was one of the earliest American practitioners of the short story and is generally considered the inventor of the detective fiction genre. He is also credited with contributing to the emerging genre of science fiction.

Edgar secretly married his 13-year-old cousin, but tragedy struck in 1843 when his wife contracted tuberculosis, the disease that had already claimed his mother, brother, and foster mother. His wife died at age of 20.

The January, 1845 publication of "The Raven" made Edgar Allan Poe a household name. He died at the age of 40. Throughout a career marked by poverty and the deaths of those closest to him, Edgar Allan Poe overcame adversity to become one of the greatest American writers ever.

Affirmation: I meet the challenges of life head-on.

To think about:

1. Edgar worked his way out of poverty. How important are material possessions to being successful?

2. Edgar Allan Poe overcame a difficult childhood, yet was a happy individual. How do you stay happy when you are faced with numerous setbacks?

3. Edgar Allan Poe expected life to be happy. How do you expect life to be happy in the future?

Man's real life is happy, chiefly because he is ever expecting that it soon will be so.
-Edgar Allan Poe

Resources

Introduction

Bruner, J. (1990). Culture and human development: a new look. *Human Development*, 33.

Parkin, M. (2010). More Tales for Trainers, *Using stories and metaphors to influence and encourage learning.* PA:Philadelphia. Kogan Page.

Simmons. A. (2007). *Whoever Tells the Best Story Wins, How to use your own stories to communicate with power and impact.* NY: NY. Amazon.

Across The Channel

Bio.True Story. *Gertrude Ederle.* http://www.biography.com/people/gertrude-ederle-9284131

Bad Luck Can Kick You Forward

Lost Manuscripts. http://lostmanuscripts.com/2010/07/31/hemingways-lost-suitcase/

Believe and Lead

Bio.True Story. *Winston Churchill.* http://www.biography.com/people/winston-churchill-9248164

Churchill Centre. http://www.winstonchurchill.org/

Believe, Believe, Believe

Billy Mills Profile. http://www.runningpast.com/billy_mills.htm

Stanbrough, M. (2013). *Motivational Moments in Men's Track and Field.* KS: Emporia, Roho Publishing.

Best Effort

Coach John Wooden. http://www.coachwooden.com/

Blind and In Prison

Poetry Foundation. http://www.poetryfoundation.org/bio/john-milton

Bouncing Back

The Charles Goodyear Story.
http://www.goodyear.com/corporate/history/history_story.html

Breaking Through Barriers

Stanbrough, M. (2013). *Motivational Moments in Men's Track and Field.* KS: Emporia, Roho Publishing.

Bulb Burns Bright
    Bio.True Story. *Thomas Edison*. http://www.biography.com/people/thomas-edison-9284349

Composing a Masterpiece
    Bio.True Story. *Ludwig van Beethoven*. http://www.biography.com/people/ludwig-van-beethoven-9204862

Crazy Horse
    A memorial for Crazy Horse 64 years in the making ... so far
    http://www.cnn.com/2012/11/05/us/crazy-horse-memorial/

Desire to Serve
    WIC Biography Golda Meir. http://www.wic.org/bio/gmeir.htm

    Wisconsin Historical Society. www.wisconsinhistory.org/topics/meir/

Determination
    Roebling Museum. http://roeblingmuseum.org/about-us/john-a-roebling/

    The Brooklyn Bridge, A World Wonder.
    http://www.brooklynbridgeaworldwonder.com/john-roebling.html

Dream For A World of Hope
    The Terry Fox Foundation. http://www.terryfox.org/TerryFox/Terry_Fox.html

    The Canadian Encyclopedia. *The Courage of Terry Fox*.
    http://www.thecanadianencyclopedia.com/en/article/terry-fox/

Father's Love
    Team Hoyt. http://www.teamhoyt.com/

    Keagey, B. *Winning The Race*. Healthy Living Made Simple. July/August 2013. SamsClub.com/healthy living.

Find A Way
    Diana Nyad. http://www.diananyad.com/

    Sloane, M. Hanna, J, and Ford, D. *Never, ever give up:' Diana Nyad completes historic Cuba-to-Florida swim*. http://www.cnn.com/2013/09/02/world/americas/diana-nyad-cuba-florida-swim/

Gazelle
    Stanbrough, M. (2013). *Motivational Moments in Women's Track and Field*. KS: Emporia, Roho Publishing.

Golden Arches
    Elliott, A. C. (1998). *A Daily Dose of the American Dream.* TN:Nashville. Rutledge Press.

    The Ray Kroc Story.
    http://www.mcdonalds.com/us/en/our_story/our_history/the_ray_kroc_story.html

Hard Work Reaps Rewards
    Elliott, A. C. (1998). *A Daily Dose of the American Dream*. TN:Nashville. Rutledge.

    Leadership the Marian Way. https://sites.google.com/site/leadershipthemarionway/about

    Moran, A. (1995). *Prescription for Success, The Life and Values of Ewing Marian Kauffman.* MO: Kansas City. Andrews and McNeel.

Helping Through Medical Discoveries
    BBC History Louis Pasteur.
    http://www.bbc.co.uk/history/historic_figures/pasteur_louis.shtml

I Am An Alcoholic
    Bill Wilson. http://agilewriter.com/Biography/Billwilson.htm

I Can Do Something
    Bio.True Story. *Helen Keller.* www.biography.com/people/helen-keller-9361967?page=4

    Keller, H. (1996). The Story of My Life. NY: NY. Dover Publications.

I Have A Dream
    Bio.True Story. *Martin Luther King.* www.biorgraphy.com/people/marint-luther-king-jr-9365086?page =6

Imagination Runs Wild
    All About Dr. Seuss. http://www.catinthehat.org/history.htm

    Poetry Foundation. *Theodore Geisel.* http://www.poetryfoundation.org/bio/theodor-geisel

Iron Man
    Stanbrough, M. (2013). *Motivational Moments in Men's Track and Field.* KS: Emporia, Roho Publishing.

I Will Do My Best
    Rowan, E.L. (2005). *To Do My Best: James E. West and the History of the Boy Scouts of America.* Las Vegas International Scouting Museum

Keeping the Faith
Bio.True Story. J.K. Rowling. www.biography.com/people/jk-rowling-40998?page=2

Keep on Knocking
  ColonelSanders.com. http://colonelsanders.com/history_colonelSanders.asp

Kiss of Kindness
  The Hershey Company. http://www.thehersheycompany.com/about-hershey/our-story/milton.aspx

Laughed at His Newspaper

  USA Today, 2013, April 12. *USA TODAY founder Al Neuharth dies at 89.* http://www.usatoday.com/story/news/nation/2013/04/19/al-neuharth-newspaper-founder-dies-at-89/2097995/

Leading Through Challenges
  Bio.True Story, *Franklin D. Roosevelt.* http://www.biography.com/people/franklin-d-roosevelt-9463381

Learning is Relative
  Einstein. http://einstein.biz/

  Nobelprize.org. http://www.nobelprize.org/nobel_prizes/physics/laureates/1921/einstein-bio.html

Life Tastes Good
  Coca Cola History: World of Coca-Cola. https://www.worldofcoca-cola.com/coca-cola-facts/coca-cola-history/

  Harvey. P. (1977), Paul Harvey' The Rest of the Story. NY: NY. Bantam Books

Long Walk to Freedom
  Bio.True Story. *Nelson Mandela.* www.biography.com/people/nelson-mandela-9397017" page 4

  Mandela. N. (1995). *Long Walk to Freedom.* NY: NY. Little, Brown and Company.

Making A Difference
  Nobelprize.org. http://www.nobelprize.org/alfred_nobel/biographical/articles/life-work/

Mistakes May Turn Out Well
  Harvey. P. (1977), *Paul Harvey's The Rest of the Story.* NY: NY. Bantam Books

  Potato chip. http://www.snopes.com/business/origins/chips.asp

Mount Everest - I'm Still Growing
  James S. Huggins' Refrigerator Door.
  http://www.jamesshuggins.com/h/mot1/hillary_growing.htm

Music Genius
Bio.True Story. *Ray Charles.* www.biography.com/peole/rau=cjar;es-9245001?page =2

Never Too Late

NY Times. Dec. 14, 1961. *Grandma Moses Is Dead at 101*; Primitive Artist 'Just Wore Out. *http://www.nytimes.com/learning/general/onthisday/bday/0907.html*

O'Brien. E. (2008). *Great Lives from History: The 20th Century Grandma Moses.* http://salempress.com/Store/samples/great_lives_from_history_20th/great_lives_from_history_20th_moses.htm

No Limits
Break Your Shackles. http://breakyourshackles.com/lawofattraction/self-esteem-and-confidence/accept-limits/

Overcoming Dyslexia
Dyslexia Help. www.dyslexiahelp.umich.edu/success-stories/tom-cruise

Good Learners: www.goodlearners.net/TomCruise.html

Persistence of Lincoln
Lincoln Never Quits. http://www.rogerknapp.com/inspire/lincoln.htm

Playing With One Hand
Bernotas, B. (1995). *Nothing to Prove: the Jim Abbott Story.* NY: NY. Kodansha American.

Real Horror Story
Rogak, Lisa. (2009). *Haunted Heart: The Biography of Stephen King.* NY: NY. St. Martin's Press

Revolutionary Vision
The Henry Ford. http://www.thehenryford.org/

Rough Road to Success
Bio.True Story. *Oprah Winfrey.* http://www.biography.com/people/oprah-winfrey-9534419

Rough Rider
Bio.True Story. *Theodore Roosevelt.* http://www.biography.com/people/theodore-roosevelt-9463424

Soul Surfer
Bethany Hamilton. http://bethanyhamilton.com/
Soul Surfer: Bethany Hamilton. http://bethanyhamilton.com/

Starry Starry Night
    Van Gogh Gallery. http://www.vangoghgallery.com/misc/biography.html

Successful Act
    Academy Achievement Sydney Poitier.
    http://www.achievement.org/autodoc/page/poi0bio-1

    Sydney Poitier Biography. http://www.imdb.com/name/nm0001627/bio

Trailblazing
    Sam Walton. http://corporate.walmart.com/our-story/heritage/sam-walton

    Walton, S. (2007). *Sam Walton Made In America: My Story.* NY: NY. Random House.

Triumph of An American Dreamer
    Amazing Story of Young Walt Disney. www.chase-adream.com.achieving_greatness.html

    Conversations With Walt Disney. http://blogiqmatriz.com/walt-disney

This Seat Is Mine
    Bio.True Story. *Rosa Parks.* www.biography.com/people/rosa-parks-94433715

Turning Bad Luck Into Good Luck
    Walgreens. http://www.walgreens.com/marketing/about/press/facts/fact3.jsp

Unlock Your Mind
    The Life of Harry Houdini. http://www.thegreatharryhoudini.com/

Wear The Red
    Marshall, J. (2002). *The Lakota Way Stories and Lesson for Living.* NY: NY. Penguin Compass.

Wonder of It All
    Stevie Wonder Official Site. http://www.steviewonder.net/

World's Toughest Race
    The Remarkable Story of Cliff Young. http://paddyupton.com/newsletter/the-remarkable-story-of-cliff-young/

While I Pondered Weak and Weary
    Bio.True Story. *Edgar Allan Poe.* http://www.biography.com/people/edgar-allan-poe-9443160

    Poe Museum. www.poemmuseum.org/life.php

About the Author

Dr. Mark Stanbrough is a professor in the Department of Health, Physical Education and Recreation at Emporia State University in Kansas. He teaches graduate and undergraduate exercise physiology and sports psychology classes and is the director of Coaching Education. The Coaching Education program at Emporia State is currently one of only ten universities in the United States to be accredited by the National Council for the Accreditation of Coaching Education. He was a co-founder of the online physical education graduate program, the first in the United States to go completely online. He received his Ph.D. in exercise physiology from the University of Oregon, and undergraduate and master's degrees from Emporia State in physical education. He has served as department chair and has served on the National Association for Sport and Physical Education National Sport Steering Committee and is a past member of the board of directors for the National Council for the Accreditation of Coaching Education.

Mark has over thirty years of coaching experience at the collegiate, high school, middle school and club level. Coach Stanbrough served eight years as the head men's and women's cross country/track and field coach at Emporia State (1984-1992) with the 1986 women's cross country team finishing second at the NAIA national meet. He has also coached at Emporia High School and Glasco High School in Kansas. He is a Level I and II USATF certified coach. Mark has served as the USATF Missouri Valley Association President and as the head referee at numerous national meets. He is a member of the Emporia State University Athletic Hall of Honor and the Health, Physical Education, Recreation Hall of Honor and has won numerous coach-of-the-year awards at the high school and collegiate levels.

www.ingramcontent.com/pod-product-compliance
Lightning Source LLC
Chambersburg PA
CBHW081501040426
42446CB00016B/3343